DANIEL WAS HERE

C L CABRERA

To my boyfriend. This story came a long time before you. I thought I'd created a world where a Mexican girl with a hard life could fall for a Jewish boy from the other side of the country. I didn't realize until I met you that I lived in that world already.

CONTENT WARNINGS

- Drugs
- Alcohol
- Smoking
- Politics
- Domestic Violence
- Chronic Illness
- Medical Treatments
- Mentions Solicitation of a Minor
- Death, Dubious Consent
- Age Gap (Younger MMC)

DAY 792

11/3/1983

Home Sweet Home. I read the hand-embroidered sign hanging above our sink as I waited for my coffee. *Home Sweet Home*. I found the sign leaning against a garbage can as I walked to the bus stop. When I saw that framed piece of fabric, I knew I needed its message in this room. I carried that thing to work and back, it rode in the seat next to me, twice. I smiled as I ran my fingers along the counter. *My home*. I've come so far, now all we had to do was figure out how to make it sweet.

The bottom step of the stair creaked and I forgot about the coffee. *Time to go*. I needed my purse and my coat. I rushed to the coat closet. My purse strap made it over my shoulder before I felt him standing behind me.

"You didn't say goodbye." Rob kissed my neck, his hand finding my hair as he pulled me closer. Strands ripped from their roots. I winced, hating the way his mustache scratched, how his smile imprinted on my skin.

"Yesterday morning, I pissed you off by waking you." I

shrugged him away, and turned around. My hands came up to guard my face from his mood, my fingers splayed wide. *It's time to go.*

"Why are you such a bitch? I just wanted to say good morning." He raised the question as he gripped my shoulder, preventing me from walking away.

Too dumb to keep my mouth closed, I said the second meanest thing to come to mind. "Why are you a prick?" My hands fell to his chest and I pushed.

His brows came together, his lips curled, and his fist landed at the apex of my abdomen, a marble ball of knuckles and insecurity.

I stumbled into the wall, the blow forcing the air from my lungs as he leaned in close.

"You make me so mad." His clenched teeth distorted his words. His fisted hands pressed into the wall, trapping me.

Sliding down, I tried to breathe. The tingling in my lips reminded me of the pressure of his grip on my throat and our last fight. I needed to escape before his fingers snaked around my neck again. I collapsed onto my hands and knees and scrambled away.

He laughed and his foot connected with my ass.

I face-planted into the faded linoleum of the kitchen. One of my arms lifted for protection, as I kicked at him. "Dammit, Rob! I'm going to be late for work." Drops of blood fell from my nose onto my uniform darkening the pink fabric.

He looked at the stains. This is where he draws the line. He didn't like to see me bleed. He performed his shrug-denial-dance that always preceded his apologies, his mouth hanging open, his arms dangling at his sides. I didn't wait for one slack-jawed excuse; I bolted, scooping up my shoes as I went.

The slamming door echoed down the empty alleyway. I ran past the parked cars and graffitied garage doors behind our block of row houses, circling onto the sidewalk. With every footfall of my burning feet, my body jolted, and my head throbbed. The cold didn't touch me at first: my heart pumped too hard, my mind raced too fast. I crumpled onto the bus-stop bench, the dry air burning my lungs, my hands finding my chest as it rose and fell.

My slowing breaths became white clouds, and my wet hair hardened into stalactites. I distracted my mind from the temperature with frivolous tasks, scrubbing the bloodstains on my shirt with spit and combing my fingers through my hardened hair. Finally, I lifted my naked feet to rub the numbness away.

I can't believe I pushed him.

My watch told me the bus would be here in an hour. *Three AM?* I shook my head. *Will I freeze to death before then?*

The lamps above glared off the ice formed at the corners of that Philadelphia morning. My balanced South Street neighborhood glinted under a layer of frost, and my tear-filled vision blended the reds and browns of the brick into muddy walls promising shelter. I pulled on my shoes and jerked my knees to my chest, conserving heat.

I never expected to end up here, surrounded by gray skies and concrete. Named after an ancient civilization of Central America, endless skies and age-old customs romanced me, leaving me yearning for distant times. Before my mother died, she told me stories about the Mayan people.

Maya, she said, *they created gigantic buildings that doubled as calendars. They were fearless and so are you, mija.*

Often, when I'm cold, I imagine their hot lands and painted faces. If only I could claim their ruthlessness and forethought as my own.

"Ma'am?"

I turned, surprised to find a teenager standing behind me. "Yes?"

His tight auburn curls formed a halo on his head, and a strong cleft chin added an edge of seriousness. He held out a wool blanket. "I saw you without a coat." He pointed at his second-floor window and smiled. His wide mouth and full lips, generous with his attention.

Taking the proffered blanket, I smoothed my skirt. A sigh escaped my chest as I settled the wool over my shoulders. I tucked it around my waist and legs, lifting it over my head and covering up the blood spots, torn stockings, makeup-less face in quick motions.

"Thank you." Chattering teeth broke my words.

He sat next to me, and I forced myself not to scoot away. "Can I get you anything else? I can make some coffee."

I shrugged, my eyes narrowing as I glared at him. "What do you want?"

"Nothing, I guess I was bored." He tilted his head. "I don't sleep."

"You don't?" I asked, apprehension building. He smelled like mint cough drops. There was something wrong with this guy.

"Life's too short for sleep." He took off his glove. "I'm Daniel. Daniel Eppstein." He lifted his hand as if to shake mine.

I stared down at it. *Was this kid joking?* "I'm Maya." Frowning, I opted out of the handshake.

"Well, nice meeting you." Daniel stood. "I'll leave you to yourself."

Suddenly, I didn't want him to leave. "Wait." I pulled the blanket tight around my shoulders. "What about this thing?"

"Keep it."

"But?"

He waved his hand, that smile returning as our eyes met. "Don't worry about me. You just stay warm."

Don't cry. Don't cry. Don't cry. I watched him leave, tears blurring my vision as I clung to the kindness he'd left behind.

DAY 791

11/4/1983

I walked to the bus stop in silence the next day, happy to have slipped out of the house unnoticed. A Skor bar sat on the counter when I woke, and I cracked it open on my way to the bus stop. Rob's apologies always tasted like chocolate.

Even as children, he handed me the melted end of his Charleston chew after pulling my pigtails. It started with those innocent little hurts and grew into broken bones and stitches. I didn't hate Rob for his lack of control or heavy hand. Maybe because I watched the world beat those traits into him. Our path out of homelessness shaping him into the affectionate bully who served Philadelphia's hardcore with their drugs of choice; leaving me to be his static punk princess, a pretty thing to show off and pay the bills when dealing went from feast to famine.

I sucked at the toffee stuck to my teeth as I shoved the wrapper in my pocket. My angel from yesterday sat at the bus stop.

"I don't have your blanket. I wanted to wash it." I yawned as I took a seat next to him.

Daniel smiled, waving the statement away as he held out a steaming mug of coffee. "You want?"

"Totally." Taking the cup to warm my hands, I took in a breath of the rich smell and let myself smile. "So tell me what a kid is doing saving damsels in distress at all hours of the night?"

"I'm not a kid, I just don't get out much. And I'm up this late because nighttime is the best time to read." His nervous laugh emphasized his awkwardness.

"Rad, what are you reading?"

With his hands free of the coffee, they float around as if they've lost their tether. "*The Princess Bride*."

I laughed. "That's a good one. What school assigns William Goldman?"

"I'm homeschooled." He studied my face. "You look different with makeup on."

"I'm sure I do. You look different when I'm not so cold." I held the coffee cup to my chest. "How old are you?" I searched his cherub face for signs of age. He was probably a year or two my junior, but his air of innocence left me thinking of him as a boy as if innocence always equaled ignorance.

"How old are you?"

I gasped and clutched my shirt with mock offense. "Hella rude, you're never supposed to ask a woman her age."

"Then age doesn't matter." He folded his gloved hands together.

I narrowed my eyes as I analyzed this kid's strangeness. "You're a little perv, aren't you?" I came up with no alternative explanation.

"I've never been called that." He raised his hand to his cheek, his lips tightening with an expression between a smile and a frown. Amusement and offense playing tug-a-war with his face. "Sorry, I'm not used to talking to girls."

I snorted. "I guess that's what happens when you don't get to practice at school."

"I guess so." His hand returned to his lap, his back straightening. "I wish I were in school."

"That's what books are for, right?" I patted him on the back, my chest tightening when he didn't answer. "High school wasn't for me either." I shrugged. "Life has taught me enough."

His lips flattened, and he leaned back to look at me. "Life has a way of teaching the hard stuff, doesn't it?"

Our eyes connected, his honey browns framed with sweetness and dark lashes. *What could he know about hard stuff? He had a home. He had parents to educate him and a house to live in. What else do we need?*

"Are you going to drink that coffee?" Daniel asked, as he looked away.

"I don't think so." I handed the mug back. "Honestly, I already had two cups."

He took a sip and stuck out his tongue, his brows furrowing. "This stuff tastes like crap, anyway."

"You should head back inside before you catch a cold," I said, doing my best not to laugh.

Those light eyes found mine again. "It was fun hanging out." He paused before standing. "We should do this again sometime. I'll loan you a book."

"I live at the library."

He raised his brows and paused. "But, I have great taste. You have to let me pick a few out for you."

"'As you wish.'"

He grinned. I waved and nodded and waved again, catching his smile reflected on my face.

DAY 790

11/5/1983

I knocked on Daniel's door as I searched my memory for his surname. *Eperstein? No. Eppton? No. Epperton. Yeah that's it. Daniel Epperton.*

A slight woman with mousy hair and lines around her eyes pulled the door open.

"Mrs. Epperton." I lifted the folded blanket. "Your son lent me this the other day."

"So close, I'm Mrs. Eppstein." A smile spread across her face, and I saw my Angel's cheeks. She took the blanket and opened the door further. "Come in, come in! Daniel told me all about you." She waved me in with her fluttering hands. Their house smelled like baked cookies.

Books lined the living room wall, and I spotted a handful of the classics I recognized intermingled with an arrangement of technical books about law. I took a seat, folding my hands as I sank into the divan; distracted from my reading by its softness.

Mrs. Eppstein remained standing. "Would you like

anything to drink? Are you hungry? Can I get you anything?" Her clipped words raced after each other. "Sorry, I'm nervous. I have a question for you. I need to get this out." Her hands planted on her hips. "I want to offer you a job."

"A job?" I asked, shocked to have been invited in to begin with.

"A job, cleaning my house. My husband and I are both working full-time. Between that and homeschooling our son, I'm swamped. Daniel pointed out that if I had help around the house, I'd have more time for his schooling. He thinks you are trustworthy."

"He's nice." My skin remembered the feel of the wool blanket I returned. "He was a lifesaver the other day."

"Yes, yes, that's his way." She waved the topic away, speaking with her hands with the same mannerisms as Daniel. "What do you think? Will you do it? You can come when your schedule allows. We'd pay you well."

I didn't have experience interacting with parental figures, so I mimicked Daniel, standing and holding out my hand. "That sounds radical."

She scrunched her nose at my word, a smile creeping over her cheeks, and once again, Daniel lived in her face.

DAY 788

11/7/1983

Friday nights among the mohawks and raised fists of the Philadelphia hardcore revitalized me. My weekends submerged in Philly's underground punk scene kept me going through the hardest weeks. Caught up in a wave of incited youth, I lolled into an intoxicated dance. The crowd's smells intertwined, our bodies pressed into a single mass–our hearts hammered to the beat of the resentment boiling below the surface of our city's concrete facade.

"I'll never follow you!" We screamed with the band, our voices rising as if the stage and the crowd were on opposing sides. Our irreverence and shamelessness reminded me of the freedom I did not have at home. Away from the chains of Rob and my sixty-hour work week, I became Maya, the warrior. A girl who shouted loud and proud. The burn of activism heated my body, and I welcomed the fire.

Hours later, six of us stumbled from the building, our faces burning with the afterglow of vented frustrations and mosh pit havens. The promise of boos and a good high drew us to our next destination.

"F.O.D. was bitchin' tonight." Rob walked backward as he referred to Flag of Democracy, a punk show staple. "But you were better." His smile half-buried in his facial hair, he held out his arms for the band, as if to gather them up in a group hug.

The lead singer laughed, his fingers running over the shaved side of his head. "Not even."

Soon Rob arrived at our stoop and turned on his heels, leading us up the steps. "I've got something special for you guys." His brow waggled as he hinted at whatever type of reefer he planned on selling them. "Let's get inside before everyone else shows up." He clapped his hands, rubbing them together.

Rob owned every warm body that entered our house. He reigned over our after-parties like a king who ruled with political schmoozing. I squirmed as he boasted and postured, his arm finding its way around me every time I tried to slip away. His years of street fights and lifting chiseled into his posture.

After my third try, his toe tapped, and beads of sweat collected on his forehead. He leaned down as if to kiss my ear. "Why are you trying to leave me?" The wetness of his clenched teeth touched my ear.

"I want everyone to be comfortable." I smiled for our guest's benefit. "You know, be a good host." *Please don't cause a scene. Please don't cause a scene.*

"Good idea. Can you grab me a beer?"

I nodded, and he smacked my ass as I walked away. His hand jolted me forward and I winced at his quick movement, at his strength.

In the kitchen, I took a swig from the first fifth I came

across. The brown liquid made me wince as I swallowed it. The glass clinked against the counter as I left the bottle behind to search for better company. Passing familiar faces with piercings and Mohawks, I gravitated to a woman who sat by herself at the edge of the dining room.

"Hi, I'm Maya." I settled into the chair next to her.

"Cheryl." She smelled like rose perfume. Her perm matched her cardigan, making her the most ordinary-looking girl in the house. "I'm from DC. I took winter quarter off from school and my friend got me a job at the community college." A rich girl, slummin' it. "She's the reason I'm here. We came with her boyfriend, but they ditched me." She pointed out the offenders through the fog of cigarette smoke. The couple curled around each other, their tongues so far down the other's throat I couldn't tell where one head started, and the other ended.

Cheryl shrugged, her fake curls bouncing. "Like, they always do this." Pulling a pack of cigarettes from her purse, she set one on her lip. "Want one?"

"Nah." I shook my head.

"How about you? How'd you get mixed up in this crowd?"

"This is my place." I pointed at the ceiling. "But I'm not from here either. I grew up in Tennessee."

She frowned, her face revealing she expected a different answer. Her eyes lingered on my skin as if to decide where on the brown side of ochre it belonged. "I wouldn't have guessed." She let out a pretty laugh as she lit the end of her cigarette. "You don't look like you're from here?" Her explicit question was obvious: 'you're not from the states, are you?'

"I was born in Tennessee, but my parents were from California. Is that what you mean?"

Her brows rose as if she wanted to continue her interrogation.

"What do you do at the community college?" I did my best to keep a straight face as I changed the subject.

The distraction worked, her eyes lit up. "I administer tests, you know, like the GED."

"The GED."

"It's the high school equivalency exam, it works like a diploma on your resume."

My head spun with the possibilities. I opened my mouth, but she spoke first.

"I just needed to get away from DC." She squinted at her friend and frowned. "The politics and the backstabbing. It's bogus over there." She waved her cigarette at the couple, its cherry glowing in a bright arch. "You guys might all be pissed-off here, but at least you people still neck."

I tore my eyes away from the pornographic scene in the room's corner, not ready for the change in subject. "People don't neck in DC?"

"People get screwed over, but that's about it." She smirked.

I reached for something positive about DC and thought of my last day at work. The smell of breakfast and the constant mumble of the news in the background as I served plates.

"What about Martin Luther King Day?" I asked.

"What day?" She turned away from the couple, giving me her full attention.

"Martin Luther King Day." I scooted to the edge of my chair. "I think I saw something on the news about the nation honoring Martin Luther King Jr?" I remembered the announcement coming from the White House Rose Garden.

"Gag me with a spoon." Her nose wrinkled as she interrupted my thoughts. "Reagan thinks if he throws civil rights leaders a party once a year, we will forget his stance on the Voting Rights Act. Like, he's heinous." She folds her arms around her waist. "Sometimes, I consider moving to Canada. I can't believe we have to deal with his lame-ass for two more years."

I nodded, distracted by a hand tightening on my shoulder. I didn't have to look up to know Rob wore a charming smile over his set jaw.

"Maya, I thought I lost you." Bruises bloomed under his fingers. "Who's this?" He held a drink out to me with his other hand.

"Uh, Rob." I took the red cup. "Umm, this is Cheryl."

"Hello, Cheryl." He took a seat on the ground in front of us, his legs crossed, one knee touching my leg and the other touching hers. "You don't look like you belong here."

Cheryl transformed, her cheeks turning pink and her lashes fluttering. "I don't belong here." Her eyes took their time studying Rob's bad boy features, pausing at his facial, his leather jacket, and his ripped jeans.

Rob leaned forward, his hand resting on her thigh. "Maya always finds the prettiest girls at the party."

She blushed, and I gulped down my drink all at once.

Rob turned to me. "Don't you think?"

"Yeah, Rob, why don't you fuck her and get it over with?" I stumbled out of my seat, tripping over Rob as I went.

"Watch out, Maya, someone might notice you're on the rag."

I lifted my middle finger as I headed to the kitchen.

DAY 787

11/8/1983

I fell asleep on the couch after drinking too much to make it up the stairs. The sound of the shower running woke me and a headache sent stars flying in the darkness of my skull. I pressed my fist against my forehead, my eyes letting in light in small tentative blinks. Cups and cigarette butts littered the living room.

The sun peeked in around the window shade, and I wondered when Rob cleared everyone out this morning and why he was in the shower. That man took whole days to recover from a party. I squeezed my eyes shut and rubbed at my face as I rolled onto my back.

I ignored the sound of creaking stairs, hoping Rob would assume I was asleep. The joints of the front door opened with a squeal and I glimpsed Cheryl's cardigan and wet curly hair as she snuck out. My eyes stung. Rob and I had our problems, but this hadn't been one of them.

I rolled off the couch with a grunt and followed Cheryl. My day-old clothes smelled like smoke and rum, and concert. I winced away from the sun as I searched the sidewalks for a cardigan. She made her way toward South Street proper. I heard the horns and brakes of the busy street from a block away. She'd be safe enough in this neighborhood, but she'd probably get lost.

"Cheryl."

Either she ignored me or she couldn't hear me, because she continued to march in the opposite direction. I hurried in my pursuit, passing the row houses that often reminded me of library books and how their heights never matched when shelved.

"Cheryl, wait up."

She shook her head as I caught up to her. "I didn't know. Not until he called me 'Maya' this morning."

"That's. Not. Why. I'm. Here." I gasped between each word, feeling the alcohol escaping my lungs as I caught my breath.

"What do you want?"

I kept pace with her. "I haven't slept with Rob in months. I want to leave him."

"Good, because he scared me." She held her wrist as she stopped walking.

"I want to ask you about the GED."

She smiled, her shoulders lifting. "Help me find the subway and I'll tell you all about it."

DAY 786

11/9/1983

Mrs. Eppstein opened the door to let me in as I lifted my hand to knock.

"Welcome, Maya. Can I call you Maya?"

"Yes, ma'am," I said, following her through the living room and into the kitchen.

"It's a horrible mess in here." She waved at the single dish in the olive-green kitchen sink. Then, she opened the closet door and pointed inside. "The mop and broom are here. Most of the detergents are under the kitchen sink, along with the sponges and the scrub brush."

"Thanks, Mrs. Eppstein."

"I want to show you how I do things before you get started." She spent the better half of an hour explaining her organization and cleaning techniques. Her pale hands flew about like trapped doves looking for an escape, and I watched transfixed.

At age eight, a fire took my mother. What she taught me

about housekeeping came down to one memory—helping her wash the dishes—the smell of the bubbles, the feel of the warm water, laughter. Daniel's mother approached chores differently. She showed me how to clean places I didn't know needed washing, her face taut and severe.

"Wash your hands before and after each project. It helps us all stay healthy." First, she washed between her fingers and scrubbed her palms. Then she rubbed the suds up to her wrists and around her thumbs. Her white hands turned red, as did my cheeks. My turn—my chest tightened as I ran hands the color of the ancient earth under the water. I felt like a heathen next to this woman.

"Well." she smoothed her skirt. "I should probably head out."

"You have a lovely home." I picked up the towel and dried my hands. "I hope I can do this as well as you."

"I don't expect you to," she said as she took one step toward the living room and then another. Her eyes flitted to the clock; her ever-busy hands found each other and knotted at her waist. "Are you sure you're okay with all this?"

I nodded

"You're confident you can do this?"

This time I paused before nodding, studying her eyes. "I'll do my best."

She sighed, looking away. "It's hard to let go." She waved at the kitchen and then her house.

"I bet." My lips tightened, and I reached into my past feelings of lost control. My throat constricted as if Rob's hands wrapped around it. I blew away the discomfort and decided it would be best to distract her. "Where did you want me to start?"

"How about you do the kitchen floors today? And maybe the bathroom? I have to run some errands, and when I get back, I'll write up a schedule for you." She nodded as she spoke, one foot exiting the kitchen.

"Bye." I waved, my other hand held my elbow.

"Goodbye. Thank you."

I heard the front door close as I put the mop bucket in the sink.

Sweat ran down my face as I scrubbed, the saltiness burning my eyes. I gave each nook attention. After round one with soap, I switched to the mop. I jumped when I heard someone step into the kitchen behind me.

"Maya?" A breakthrough falsetto hitched Daniel's question mark. He cleared his throat. "What are you doing here?"

I picked up the mop. "Cleaning. Your mom said it was your idea." I pointed at the linoleum where he stood. "I scrubbed that."

His eyes widened, and he stepped back onto the carpet. "Sorry."

"Sorry?" I smiled. "I kid you not. You're an angel."

He blushed, opened his mouth, closed it, and shook his head.

"What?"

"I, uh . . . I was being selfish." He combed his curls with his fingers. "I wanted to see you again."

My palms sweat as I tried on Daniel's bravery. "That's rad, 'cause I wanted to see you too."

"Do you want some help?" He started rolling up his

sleeves. His ever-present blush made my heart skip. "I bet she has you doing the bathroom next?"

"You don't have to clean, but I wouldn't mind your company." Our eyes locked and I looked away first.

DAY 785

11/8/1983

I wore my diner uniform as I knocked, waiting for several minutes before a breathless Daniel opened the door. Mrs. Eppstein's welcome the day before was the opposite of what I experienced today.

He wiped a layer of sweat from his brow. "Sorry, I lost track of time." He bent over, wheezing, as he held the door open.

I stepped into the entryway, eyeing him as wheezing became a cough, and then returned to panting. "Where's your mom?"

"She doesn't get home until seven, and Dad, well, he'll be later than that." He shut the door behind me and dug a note out of his pocket. "But here, mom left this list." Daniel handed over the crumpled piece of paper.

She'd listed ten chores, eight of which someone had crossed out. "So what's with these?" I pointed at one through eight, with the line striking through them.

He blushed, smiled, and then ran his fingers through his

hair. "Those are the ones I did already," his smile widened in response to my slacked-jawed surprise. "I finished up number nine." He pointed at the list, saying *Move books from the second-floor guestroom to the third-floor library.* That explained his heavy breathing.

"You know your mom is paying me to do those things, right?" I asked.

"I see it as a list of things she wants to do." He rubs at his chest with his fist. "She's paying you for your time." he clears his throat, still rubbing his chest. "Well, I was hoping to propose using that time for something else?"

I took a step back and raised my hands. "Hey kid, I'm not sure what bogus ideas you've got in your head, but I'm not—"

"I'm not a kid and I want you to teach me to drive." His cheeks reddened as I shook my head.

"You are a kid, look, you're asking me to teach you to drive?"

"We are probably the same age." He pointed at me. "And, yes. That's it, teach me to drive."

"No can do. I don't even have a car." I rolled my eyes. He lived with his parents, he was a child.

"I have a car." He started digging through his pocket and produced a key. "I got it for my birthday last year but haven't driven it once. My parents are too busy. They wouldn't know the difference. I can work on my mom's to-do list, and in return, you can show me the ropes behind the wheel."

"What makes you think I know how to drive?" I couldn't keep the mischief off my face. I had to give it to him; he was pretty darn smart. He'd planned this all along.

"I saw you driving that blue truck over the weekend." He raised his brows with a smirk.

"Hmm." He'd seen me driving Rob's truck. Looking over his mother's list, I tried to decide if I cared about getting in trouble. "I'm not saying 'yes' yet. Let me dust, and we can look at this car."

Daniel hugged me. Crushing my arms against my body, he grinned, and I leaned away dazed. He let me go. I'd never suffered a more virginal hug, his body stiff, his arms awkward; but somehow, it made me feel safe.

"I have something for you."

I raised my brows as he produced three books from the end table. "*The Count of Monte Cristo*?" The title of the top book made me smile.

"These three reminded me of you."

"How does a book remind you of me?" I asked with a roll of my eyes, ignoring the pink splotches popped up at the collar of his shirt. "You don't know me."

He shrugged, and I took the books, looking at each title. *Hitchhiker's Guide to the Galaxy* and *One Hundred Years of Solitude*. "I've read this one." I handed back *The Count of Monte Cristo*. "You and your romances."

"Don't tell anyone. It will ruin my reputation." He held the book to his chest as he laughed.

We dusted together in silence. He bounced on his heels as he worked, smiling from start to finish. He washed his hands at the kitchen sink. I washed my hands, too, following his example.

"You ready to meet her?"

His mood rubbed off on me, and my lips twitched at his excitement. "Show me this car."

The clunker had a spotless interior and a boxy steel frame. "So tan is your color?" I asked as I slid into the driver's seat, smelling wax and dust.

He didn't respond, running his hands over the leather dashboard, his eyes closed.

"Okay, let's do this right." I pushed my seat back to the furthest position with a creak. "If you can name everything I point at, I will trade you seats."

Daniel rubbed the cold out of his fingers. "Deal!"

"Okay, what's this?" I pointed down to my right foot.

"The brake."

"And this?"

"The clutch." Concentration made his thick brows lower.

"What about this?" I grabbed the gearshift.

"Um, the shifter?"

"Close enough," I motioned, moving the gearshift straightforward, "and what gear would I be in now?"

"Third." He leaned forward, folding his hands together, the same way his mother did.

"Nope." I laughed as he wrinkled his nose. "Trick question." I shrugged. "I couldn't shift without pushing the clutch down."

"You got me." He beamed. One of his hands escaped its self-imposed imprisonment and landed like a butterfly on mine. Our contrasting skin tones reminded me of pearls and gold. "Thanks for taking this seriously."

"I better. If you crash and die, I'd be in big trouble."

"I won't die in a car crash," he said as his hand lifted.

DAY 779

11/16/1983

My hands became prunes as I scrubbed and rinsed the dishes. Daniel sat on the counter, a towel on his lap.

"So, what is that language I heard your mom and you speaking the other day?"

"Yiddish."

"It must be nice?" I handed him a plate.

"What?"

"Speaking two languages. I remember my parents speaking Spanish to each other, but never to me."

The faucet dripped and I passed another dish before tightening both handles. Something about Daniel made silence safe and memories painless.

"My mom wanted me to invite you to Thanksgiving."

"I thought you guys were Jewish?" I said, my head still in my parents kitchen as they argued in Spanish.

Daniel belly laughed, his arm brushed against mine. "What are you thinking about?"

"What?" I asked, my face warming as I realized what I'd said.

"Thanksgiving is an American holiday, not a religious one." He set a dry plate down. "Of course, we celebrate it."

His playfulness brought a smile back to my face. "You think that's funny?"

He nodded, his eyes still gleaming.

"Let me show you something funnier." Lifting my hands from the sink, I flicked water at him.

He slid from the counter and reached around me. His shoulder and mine created an intimate heat, my skin tingling where we met.

He scooped a handful of suds onto my shirt with raised brows and a quick smile.

I gasped, jumping back, my fingers dangling as if disgusted. "You." I glared at him.

He stuck out his tongue.

We both looked back at the sink, where a lone plastic cup floated among the bubbles.

I dove for it.

He did too. I grabbed the cup first and backed away, intending to soak him. I brandished it like a bomb, raising it above my head as if to throw it. He smiled and lunged. I danced back, still holding it aloft. The water sloshed down as we struggled, his hand coming up to my ribs, tickling me. Before I knew it, I'd run out of space, leaving me cornered between the counter and the kitchen door.

"Look what you've done," I said between laughs, my speeding heart skipping as he stepped closer.

"I've got you cornered." I didn't recognize the maturity in his voice as his hands captured my cheeks with the gentlest touch I'd ever known. His brows came together, his eyes widening as they found mine.

"What's your plan now?" I came up to my toes as if his hands lifted me with their influence.

"I'm going to—"

His cheek brushed my cheek, and my breath caught, my body stilling. His stubble against my skin drew me to him. Next, his lips placed a question against my mouth. His eyes closed, his inhalation capturing my soul.

I should have hesitated—I should have said "no," rested my hand on his chest, and pressed until the space between us became proper again. But the pull was too strong, the kiss too soft.

I opened my mouth.

My lips parted as I let his tongue in, kissing him back and dropping the cup on the ground. We ignored the splash soaking our shoes. My hands found his arms. My fingers discovered the muscles there as I pulled him closer.

His body answered, pushing mine into the door with a moan vibrating under my skin. The flutter of warmth aching between my thighs brought me back to the surface.

"Daniel," I said, my voice breathy as I pulled back. My arms fell to my sides as my mind flashed vivid images of the people who would be angry if they knew where my hands wandered.

"Yes, *ketsele*?" His half-moon eyes struggled to focus, his lips red from kissing.

"We." I took a deep breath, "this, we can't."

He stepped back, confusion on his face. "Why?" He lifted his hand to touch me, and I ducked to the side, widening the distance between us further. "I'm sorry, Maya. I thought—" he left me to finish his sentence.

"We can't do this. I shouldn't have." Folding my arms, I looked away from his tear-filled eyes and his set jaw.

He wiped at his face, turning away from me. "I'll finish up. Please go."

Rob sat in the living room, the lights off. An empty beer bottle stood on the end table. "Hey." His voice rattled from disuse.

"Hey." I flipped the light on and shucked my jacket.

"Where have you been?" Rob asked, leaning forward as he cracked his knuckles.

I peeled my wet shoes off, staying calm, even though my heart still beat in my lips. "What do you mean?"

"I mean, I came to visit you at the diner about an hour ago, and they told me you didn't work today." He stood, his lips twisting into a frown. "Lisa says you leave work on time every day." He stepped in my way. His broad chest blocked my path, his chin lifting in a challenge. "So I was wondering where you've been?"

"Bite me, Rob. I already told you." I headed for the stairs.

His hand closed like a vise around the nape of my neck. "No, Maya, you didn't." He squeezed. "Now tell me where you've been."

"You're mental. I fucking told you." I reached for his wrist, my nails sinking into the flesh.

He yanked me back, his fingers leaving bruises. "Why are you always such a bitch?" He pushed me onto the couch and kneeled in front of me, his hands trapping my thighs. "You're mad about that girl, but that's no reason for you—"

"I'm not screwing around on you."

The back of his hand flew at me and I squeezed my eyes

shut. The gold ring on his middle finger clicked against my tooth, splitting my lip. The tang of blood filled my mouth.

"Let me finish." He placed his hand back in my lap. "Sleeping with the girl from DC was a mistake. I was drunk. She was drunk. I don't want you fucking around to get back at me. I didn't do it on purpose." He caressed my leg, and I smelled beer and pot.

"I don't care where you put your dick." I lifted my chin as an offering. When a second blow didn't come, I took in a shaky breath. "I got a job cleaning a house."

He snorted. "You want me to believe that?"

"It's true."

He shook his head and stood, pacing as he popped his knuckles. "Take me there," he said, turning his back on me.

"What?"

"Get your ass up and show me." He marched over to the coat hanger and pulled on his jacket. "What are you waiting for?"

He stepped outside, and my socks soaked through with icy rain as I followed him. Rob wrapped his hand around my bicep and dragged me down the three concrete steps.

"Which way?"

I pointed toward the bus stop. His bone-breaking grip brought tears to my eyes as he dragged me forward. The Eppstein house grew closer, and I steadied my breath, wiping my face. Rob's cruelty sunk into my flesh through his tight grip, and I imagined the dungeon where Edmond, the Count of Monte Cristo, was imprisoned.

Rob knocked with four quick raps.

Daniel answered, his eyes widening with concern when they found me. "Maya, are you okay?" His hands fisted at his side.

Rob's head tilted up. Daniel stood inches taller than

him, but Rob looked less than impressed. His left leg outweighed the boy. "She fell. She's fine." Rob's grip tightened, and I nodded, covering the cut on my lip with my hand. "Now, son, can you get your dad?"

"Please, let's go ho—"

I cried out as Rob's fingers tangled in a clump of my hair, pulling my head back. I heard Daniel gasp. "Now, son, I asked you a question."

"My parents aren't home." Daniel held up his hands, his voice careful. "Please let go of her."

Rob's grip loosened, and I sighed in relief. "So tell me, does she clean your house?"

"Yes, sir." Daniel's eyes met mine and shifted to the ground.

"Thanks, ace." Rob turned to me, his false smile not reaching his eyes. He slapped my ass, speaking through clenched teeth. "Babe, you should have told me that from the beginning."

"Um, she should come inside and get cleaned up? I can walk her home after."

"Mind your business." Rob glared, his hand settling on my back, steering me away from my curly-haired angel.

"At least take this." Daniel pulled off his sweater and held it out to me. "It's freezing outside."

"Get bent."

I couldn't look at the devastation on Daniel's face as Rob pulled me away. My eyes fell to the ground, my feet dragged and tangled as tears blinded me.

DAY 771

11/24/1983

The house cleaning became my favorite part of the day. Like meditation, I scrubbed and wiped and surrendered to the mindlessness of it. I kept my conversations with Daniel short, afraid I'd lose control, and put my lips on his.

Today I scrubbed the toilet as he came to stand in the bathroom doorway, gift-wrapped box in his hand. A red ribbon tied around it. He shoved his free hand into his pocket.

"So, what are you doing for the next eight days?"

"What?" The brush in the toilet stilled so I could hear him.

"What are you doing on your vacation?"

He referred to the paid days his mother gave me off for Hanukkah. "I don't know. Maybe I'll pick up some extra shifts at the diner."

He smiled, a brown curl falling onto his forehead as he shook his head. "You're a workaholic. You know that, right?"

"Yeah, yeah." I stood and went to the sink to wash my hands.

"I got you a gift," he said, his smile widening as our eyes met through the mirror. He set the box on the counter.

"Really?" I looked at the red wrapping paper as I dried my hands.

He opened his mouth to reply but let out a short cough instead. His hands came up to cover his mouth as he coughed and coughed, his body doubling over. They continued coming, getting closer together, sounding like the rapid-fire of machine guns.

I could hear no movement of air as he gasped. He skirted me. His face grew ever redder. The fit racked his body, jerking him upward and then dropping him as he gagged between hacks. He kneeled in front of the toilet and vomited and coughed and vomited until nothing came out.

"Should I call your mother?" I stood frozen, my heart clenching with fear. It sounded like death. Finally, he collapsed sideways, leaning on the tub. Tears streaked his face, and his hands fisted at his chest as he pounded on his ribs with vengeful blows.

There's something in his lungs!

"Should I call an ambulance?" I asked when his eyes focused again and his head swiveled in my direction.

"No." Threads of his former voice remained.

"Okay. I'm going to go get you water." I turned to leave.

"No, *ketsele*, come here?" He waved me closer, patting the ledge of the tub. His breaths came in short pants. Tears streamed down his face.

I took a seat next to him, and he rested his head in my lap, his arms wrapping around my calves. His body shook as he clung to me. My fingers ran through his hair and I chewed my lip as I waited for his breaths to slow.

"Twenty-twenty-twenty-four hours huh-hum. Da duh-da duh sedated," I sang, the words to the Ramone song eluding me. Eventually, I gave up and hummed it to a sluggish tempo, willing the softness of my voice to heal him in a way my hands could not.

Daniel had two more fits before his mother got home. The last two were fits of intense coughing, minus the vomiting. I gripped the porcelain as he struggled, counting the seconds until he could breathe again. The helplessness brought tears to my eyes and I asked myself for the millionth time why I listened to him when he told me not to call 911.

Daniel curled on the ground, his cheek against the cool tile, his hands wrapped around my ankles when I heard the door downstairs. I screamed. "Mrs. Eppstein!"

I heard her rush up the stairs. "Daniel?" She called for her son, a desperate edge in her voice.

"We're in the bathroom."

She found us and dropped her purse, rushing to Daniel's side. "What happened?"

"*Mamala?*" Daniel's moan made my skin crawl. She touched his cheek and then his forehead.

"*Mein tayer sin*, let's get you to bed."

He nodded in response.

It took both of us to get him on his feet.

Once in the hallway, Mrs. Eppstein waved me away. I went back to the bathroom to re-clean the toilet and wipe the floors. My unsteady hands scrubbed as I allowed myself the hiccups preceding tears, my lungs mimicking Daniel's struggle. The smell of bleach replaced the smell of sick and terror.

"Thank you for staying with him."

I dabbed at my eyes and shook my head, forcing my breaths to even out before turning to Mrs. Eppstein.

"That must have been scary for you."

I couldn't meet her eyes, so I stared at her pale hands. "Is he going to be okay?" I asked as I chewed my dry bottom lip.

"He has Cystic fibrosis. He'll never be—" She dabbed at her eyes. "Now excuse me. I'm going to check on him."

She turned to go, pausing when she saw the red present. "Oh, that's mine," I said, reaching out for it.

"Goodnight." She slipped away without giving me a chance to respond.

I thought about Daniel on my walk home, and something deep inside me hurt. I remembered his need as he held onto me, rooting itself into my bones.

My throat itched, and I wondered if I could catch his cough. I cradled his gift in my hands and resolved to see the doctor if it didn't go away in the next few days.

Once inside and alone, I settled on the couch. Gold swirls decorated the red wrapping paper. I untied the ribbon and peeled off the paper and found a small box smelling of my angel. I removed the lid and revealed a folded piece of paper; smoothing it open, I stared down at the calligraphy taking up the page.

Maya
Your name means Illusion
Like the Hindu G-ddess
The root cause of creation
They named a Japanese mountain after you
Before your birth
In Kanji Letters, you become
Truth and Reason

Night and Rain
You are the indigenous people
Of several continents,
Maya
In some languages, you are Magic
In others, you are Love
But for me
You are all of these
And so much more

My heart jumped in my chest as I read the last two lines. *And so much more.* How did he come up with this? I reread it and caught myself wiping at my cheek. The joy of flattery and the hopelessness of circumstance crowded me from either side.

DAY 769

11/26/1983

The sore throat became a cough and then a chest cold. I sat on the bed at the clinic as the Doctor listened to my lungs. The paper beneath me crinkled as I shifted.

"Your lungs sound fine. You have bronchitis." She slung her stethoscope around her neck. "I'll send my nurse back in with your prescriptions. One for cough syrup and another for antibiotics."

"You're sure it's bronchitis?" I asked, thinking about Daniel's coughing fits.

"Yes."

"So there is no chance I have cystic fibrosis?"

"No sweety, there isn't."

"I found out one of my friends has it, and I was worried—"

"Darling, you can't catch cystic fibrosis. It is something you're born with." She edged to the door with full intentions of escape.

"Oh."

"I'm sorry about your friend, though. Make sure you spend as much time with them as possible." Her hand wrapped around the doorknob. "Did you have questions?"

I shook my head.

On my bus ride home, I stopped by the library to look up cystic fibrosis. *Spend as much time with them as possible.*

After checking in with the Librarian, I headed to the section of the library I never visited. My fingers ran over the spines of books as I walked down the aisle with the section on *Genetic Conditions*. I grabbed the first Cystic Fibrosis book I found and headed to a corner to read.

Cystic Fibrosis is a genetic disorder that causes overproduction of secretions; resulting in significant issues with the lungs and gastrointestinal system. . . Their average life expectancy is fourteen-years-old.

I read on about treatments and therapies, looking at pictures and statistics. The deeper I researched, the more intense my fear. I rethought my guilt as desperation settled on my shoulders. I closed the book, deciding to teach Daniel how to drive. My heart twisted in my chest, imagining a world without him in it. *I've wasted so much time already.*

DAY 764

12/1/1983

Every cough I heard reminded me of Daniel. But my healing bronchitis left me missing him. I wandered to his house from the bus stop and, knocking on his door, checked the note I'd written him in my pocket. My response

Silence greeted me, and I turned to walk away, my arms wrapping around my ribs.

"Oh, it's you." I heard her as the door squeaked open.

"Mrs. Eppstein. I wanted to stop by—"

"I'm sorry." She patted her hair, her hands fluttering about as if they could fix the wildness of her countenance. "I can't talk right now. Daniel is at the hospital. I'm trying to pack him some clothes before I head back." Her hands settled over her mouth, the lines around her eyes deepening as they grew wet. "Oh, Maya." Her shoulders hiccuped as her breath hitched.

I looked around, wanting to hide the tears filling my own eyes–coming back to the doorway when she opened her arms in an unfamiliar invitation. I stepped into the hug of a loving mother. She cried, but that didn't stop her from holding me. I could see how Daniel's sweet soul came from hers.

We pulled apart. "Will you come upstairs with me?" she asked, wiping her eyes. "I don't want to be alone." I followed her up the steep row-house stairs as she continued to speak. "We brought him to the hospital a few hours after you left the other day. He'd been so healthy. We were all so hopeful. He wants to go to college. We thought he might . . ." She trailed off as she pushed Daniel's bedroom door open.

Daniel's room baffled me. It looked like an elderly man lived here. The smell of menthol stung my nose. Multiple packed bookshelves lined one wall, while the opposite held shelves full of futuristic-looking torture devices posed as medical equipment. On his dresser sat an assortment of pill bottles. I walked over to his bed and sat next to a duffle bag and a folded cardigan, trying not to let my surroundings crush me.

She pulled open the top dresser drawer and tossed a few pairs of socks next to me.

"Mrs. Eppstein?"

"Yes?" Her eyes focused on the tiny print of a pill bottle.

"Um. Well, the real reason I came here this morning was to let you know I appreciate you giving me this job, and--"

"Please don't tell me you're going to quit."

"Not at all. I was going to ask—" I lifted my head to meet her eyes. "Daniel showed me his car, and I was wondering if I could teach him to drive." She smiled in response, and I pushed on. "I wouldn't want you to pay me or anything. I could come one or two days a week?"

"That is a wonderful idea, Maya." Mrs. Eppstein turned away as her face once again wrinkled with sadness.

"Great, I think he'll be so excited. I'll see if he's up to it when I start cleaning again on the ninth?"

She nodded, her shoulders curled forward. I slipped the note I'd brought into one of his folded pairs of socks as I shoved them into his duffle bag.

Daniel,

You make me feel special. Thank you. Let's get back to driving again.

I've missed you,

Maya

DAY 762

12/3/1983

I waited at the door and held myself back from hugging Daniel when he opened it.

He stepped out of my way. "You came back?" he said, his voice hoarser than usual.

I studied him before answering. His gaunt face darkened with shadows since last we spoke. My eyes lingered on the bones visible at his collar and wrist. I wanted to make sure he could stay standing if I touched him.

"No doy." With a flat laugh I held my hands fisted at my sides. "I've been worried."

He frowned. "I'm sorry about that." He looked down at his feet. "I didn't mean to scare you."

I pushed his shoulder, ducking down to catch his eyes. "Did you get my note?" I smiled.

He reached into his pocket and dangled his car key between us. "I did." He smirked, and with that, the shadow of his sickness disappeared for me. I couldn't see his pallor or thinness with the brilliance of the lift in his cheeks.

"Oh, and I got you a Christmas present, too. I know it's not your holiday, but I couldn't help myself." I pulled my backpack off and started digging through it.

"We don't need a holiday for you to get me a gift." He winked. "I accept gifts all year round."

"Don't push your luck, nerd." I found the newspaper-wrapped package and held it up. "It's a keychain," I said before he could take it from my hand.

He unfolded the paper and blushed when he realized who smiled up at him from the bottle cap keychain.

I laughed as he studied the little picture of Madonna in a black corset, fishnets, and black bikini bottoms. "It's Madonna. I wasn't sure what music you liked, but I knew you liked girls, and you don't have any guy friends to give you this stuff." This time I winked.

"It's, um, well—" He cleared his throat. "It's great."

I watched him try to connect the key to the ring a few times before intervening. "Hand it over."

He grinned as he passed them to me, bouncing on his heels as he waited.

After I attached the two, I passed them back. "What do you think?"

"It's perfect." He touched my cheek, his head tilting like a question mark as if to ask if I wanted his hand there. "Thank you."

I paused, leaning into his touch, savoring the feel of his fingers. "Let's take the car for a spin?" My question sounded distant, and I closed my eyes until his hand fell away.

We waited for the car to warm up in silence, Daniel in the driver's seat, me in the passenger's. The fogged windows reminded me of other ways to produce heat, and embarrassed, I pulled my coat around me, averting my eyes.

Daniel sat straight up, adjusting his seat and then his mirrors, and once again his seat. The cold visibly bugged him. He let out a muffled cough into his shoulder, beat his chest with his fist, and cleared his throat.

Watching his nervous energy stack in layers of movement, I interrupted, out of mercy. "Okay, let's review." I watched his head lean against the headrest, his body stilling. "What do you need to do first?"

The engine purred, and rain fell. At first, one drop fell at a time, the sprinkling turning into a shower as Daniel worked his jaw.

"Maya, you know, don't you?" Daniel watched the rainfall on the windshield, the alley collecting rivers of water. "That's why you're doing this?"

"I know." I squeezed my eyes tight for a moment before turning to look at his profile. The heaviness of his brows aged him.

"So, what does that mean?" He rubbed his chest as he stared ahead. The dry air smelled of dust and Daniel's mint. "Are you doing this because you feel bad for me?"

"I'm doing this because I missed you." I cleared my throat. "And knowing you're sick made me realize you didn't have time to wait around for me to straighten my shit up." I covered my face and leaned against the dashboard, not wanting him to see the beginnings of sorrow take over my face, not wanting him to have to suffer my worry alongside his own.

"It's okay to be sad, but I don't want it to be the reason you are spending time with me." His hand stroked my back. "I've known since I was a child. This isn't new to me. You don't have to worry about me. Everyone dies; I'm just dying earlier."

Was he comforting me? With a quick pat, he lowered his hand to hover between us, palm up, and I took it. "I'm sorry." I couldn't find the words to express the heaviness in my heart. My forehead rested on his shoulder as I held my breath and tried not to cry. His hand covered mine, and I shook my head against him. "I'm so sorry."

"It's okay to be sad." He pulled me to him and held me as my shoulders moved with sobs. The warmth of his body giving me permission to feel.

We sat like this until the windows cleared and the rain lightened, neither of us having to speak to share our sorrow.

DAY 760

12/5/1983

The last two nights I couldn't sleep, those quiet circles we drove in his car replaying on the backs of my eyelids. A confusion of emotions tangled with my insides. My mind wandered into a world without Daniel and it felt like a desert. I imagined his mother and her fluttering hands. I remembered how Daniel moaned *Mamala* and counted all of the hours he was alone while his parents worked to pay for hospital bills. How many years this couple lived with the perpetual weight of a dying child.

I closed my eyes and thought of his good nature and positive attitude, the kindness guiding every word he said. Only a miracle could have brought someone out of hardship with such a sweet demeanor. I'd know, I'd grown into a ball of fury and through all of my hardships I still had hope.

His touch haunted me most. A constant pressure filled my chest and the ghost of his lips warmed mine whenever I forgot to be sad. This chemistry led me to make our plans for the day. I leaned back in my seat. "There is somewhere I want to take you." Another rainy day blurred the windshield.

"Yeah?"

"Yeah. You ready?"

He drums the steering wheel. "Let's do this."

I pointed to our right. "Rad, let's take 15th to downtown."

He turned to me as he eased the car into first, his face once again full of light. "You're going to let me drive in all that traffic?"

"How else are you going to learn?"

The drive took forever. Daniel drove like a grandmother, and I didn't complain. I'd rather he drive like a grandmother than a teenager. The city sidewalks buzzed with activity, teeming with life. Women in trousers dodged men in suits, and blue-collar workers rambled about with the gait of men who carried too much weight on their shoulders.

When and if I drove, I'd take Rob's truck. Parking that monster in the city was easier than teaching someone how to park a two-seater. After Daniel's fourth try at parallel parking, I kicked him out, promising we'd practice on a less busy street.

I slid into a spot and joined Daniel on the sidewalk as he squinted through the windows of the PSFS Building. "Have you heard about the view on the 33rd floor?" I asked.

Daniel's head tilted back, his neck craning. His eyes followed one window to the next until he came to the roof. "No, I haven't, but isn't this a bank? Will they let us in the elevator?"

"Follow my lead, kid."

He rolled his eyes. "You've got to stop calling me that, *ketsele*."

The rhythm of the foreign word as it came off his lips made me shiver. "What did you call me?"

He smirked.

I bumped him with my shoulder and grabbed his hand when he didn't reply. "Let's go."

The lobby smelled like paper money and fading cologne. Sounds echoed around the cavernous room, the sources impossible to find. I walked up to the closest bank teller, my sneakers squeaking on the marble floors.

"Can I help you?" She stared down her nose at my ripped jeans.

"Yes, ma'am, I'd like to speak to Jonathan Savage."

She raised her eyebrows at my request, looking me up and down again before she huffed away.

"Who's Jonathan?" Daniel leaned close to my ear.

I rose to my toes, drawn by the closeness of his mouth. "Umm," I said, rendered breathless by my attraction. My cheeks burned.

Daniel squeezed my hand. "What are you thinking?"

I laughed. "Nothing." I cleared my throat and tried to remember what he asked me. "Jonathan? Oh, Jonny is the bank manager. He's also the lead drummer in an Anarchy band."

He raised his brows.

"Hella ironic, right?"

Daniel nodded as Jonathan came around the corner, his three-piece suit impeccable.

"Maya." He spread his arms for a hug, and I indulged him. "What are you doing in this neck of the woods?"

"Remember when you told me you owed me one?"

"How could I forget? God, what a gnarly night."

"Well, I promised my friend here the best view of Philadelphia."

Jonathan turned to Daniel, his lips curving up in a sneaky smile. "You're in for a treat, my man." He shook Daniel's hand. "This way."

We followed Jonathan to the elevator. Once inside, he turned to me. "So spill the beans." He gestured to Daniel, "Does this mean you're leaving your wastoid of a boyfriend?"

"How's the band, Jonny?"

"You're lame. No changing the subject."

"Bite me."

The elevator dinged. Jonathan and I glared at each other, the stand-off ending as the door slid open. "Fine, we'll talk about this later." He led us to the solarium door. "You have an hour, maybe two, if you're lucky." He folds his arms.

"Thanks, Jonny." I clapped his back harder than necessary and walked past him. "Thanks for making things awkward."

"Anytime."

"Dweeb."

"Buttmunch."

"Oh, bag your face." The door shut before I finished my last insult.

"Are you guys related?"

Engrossed by the cityscape expanding before me, I jumped at the sound of Daniel's voice. "No, I've known him for a long time." My hands and forehead rested on the glass. Its iciness calmed me as it sucked away the heat of my embarrassment. I watched the sky through my lashes, the emotional whiplash of the day stalling time like the cars below with their ever flashing brake lights.

I blew a cloud of my breath against the glass and wrote with my finger, announcing in all capitals, "*DANIEL WAS*

HERE"; while I waited for the repercussions of Jonathan's questions to catch up with me.

"Why are you with Rob?"

The sound of his name in Daniel's freshly formed baritone made my shoulders tighten.I pushed back from the window. "I can give you a lot of excuses. Like, I have nowhere else to go, or he won't let me leave." I turned to Daniel, who ignored the view and studied me. "Or you could kiss me."

Like a thirty-three-story trust fall, I fell back into the sky, the glass catching me, my head tilted up. I held my breath as I watched my angel decide. His brows lifted, his lips pursed, his eyes widened. "Maya?" His forearms pressed against the glass, framing me in. "I don't think we should kiss." Those red patches formed on his cheeks. "Not if it feels wrong." His forehead rested against mine.

I closed my eyes. "One conversation won't fix my Rob-problem."

"It won't fix CF either, but that doesn't mean we pretend our problems aren't real."

I nodded against him. "I brought you here so I could kiss you." More blush spread on his face, and I couldn't help but turn until my lips found his cheek, kissing the warmth there. "Let's sit?"

I slid down the window and pulled my knees to my chest. My heart pounded as I decided which parts of my story I wanted to share. Daniel found a place across from me. Crossing his legs, he looked over my shoulder.

"Our parents died when I was eight." I cleared my throat and started over. "His parents and my parents died when we were kids. A fire took them, along with Rob's twin sisters. They were toddlers." I rubbed at my eyes even though the last time I let myself cry for them, I'd been a child.

"I'm so sorry, Maya."

I shook my head, looking down at the carpet. "It was a weird situation. We lived in a commune. Like the one in West Philly. You know, there was a police standoff a few years back." I remembered that day, seeing the black activists stand against the police had opened doors in my heart that I'd closed as a child.

"You mean MOVE?"

"The big difference is, our commune consisted of a bunch of California transplants. It had less religion and more spiritualism. You know, hippies. Oh, and mostly white people except for the few Chicanos who got swept along for the ride. Lots of families, lots of drugs. When it was good, it was fantastic. When it was bad, well. . ." I shrugged. "I don't remember a time without Rob. He helped me leave when it didn't seem safe there anymore and kept us out of the system once we were on our own."

I stood up, my body needing to move, my heart racing as I remembered getting on the bus. Rob held my hand, our sweat collecting between our palms, my teeth chattering with the cold and the intensity of the moment. The street lights flashed, brightening Rob's face. My child's brain decided I'd never be able to repay him for saving me.

"Young girls aren't treated well in the places I've come from. Girls aren't treated well anywhere in America; and if you're a Mexican-American girl, one that's not quite white or brown enough, you're fucked. But Rob always protected me. He got me out of there." I wrapped my arms around myself, the smell of the old carpet we sat on bringing me back to the present, and turned to watch a new set of rain clouds conquer my city. "Believe me when I say I've outgrown his protection. But he's not ready to give me up."

I waited for Daniel to say something, my mind bouncing from scenario to scenario, my stomach cramping with fear. I closed my eyes when his chest warmed my back, his hands following the lines of my arms until he held me.

"You are so strong." Daniel rested his cheek in my hair.

"Not strong enough." *When did my life turn into a prison? Was it the day I climbed into that bus with Rob? The day my parents died? Or when I was born?* I leaned into my angel as I counted the buildings making up the Philadelphia skyline, wondering how many prisoners of fate each of them contained, knowing if I counted, I could start with the two standing in this room.

DAY 759

12/6/1983

"Last night, I totaled up my cash and searched the newspaper classifieds for apartments and sublets." I greeted Daniel with these words. "I should have enough for my own place by February."

"Is that too long?" He asked as he closed the door behind me.

"Of course, it's too long, but I don't have a choice." I dropped my backpack on the couch and peeled off my coat. "You know, I couldn't have done this without this job."

"You would've found a way," he said.

I unwrapped my scarf and folded it. "Maybe." My flurry of movement stopped as his shoulder brushed against mine. I looked up. The grin on his face disarmed me. "Why are you smiling?"

He took my scarf and tossed it on the couch."I want to cheer you up." He raised his brows, a silent question in his eyes. "Yesterday was rough. Let's have fun today."

"Fun, huh? What kind of fun?" I rested my hands on his shoulders.

"Is that kiss you offered me still up for grabs?" He moved closer, and so did I.

"What kind of kiss did you want? Something like this?" I drew myself up to my tiptoes and kissed his nose. "Or did you have something else in mind?"

"You know." His voice rattled in his chest.

I watched his color change, returning his smile as his hands came to my waist. My heart begged for more, and my impatient fingers found his curls, pulling his face to mine. His lips to mine. His soul to mine. I breathed in his breath and explored the taste of him, reveling in the feel of his body against me. Our tongues became partners in a duet: the song, the taste of passion.

I came up for air when our lips broke apart, and he found my ear. "*Ketsele, noadnu lihiyot yakhad.*" The words burned me with their beauty, their meaning clear in the way they curled around me.

His chin traced a line down my neck, his five-o-clock shadow leaving a blazing trail behind. I tilted my head as I heaved, my breasts rising and falling and aching for his touch.

We kissed like our survival depended on it. Like our worlds would end if we did not wrap our arms around each other. This kiss spoke of life and death and all those short moments in between. An unrecognizable emotion weakened my legs and warmed my belly.

At some point, he leaned into me too hard, and we stumbled back. I caught the divan with my hand, and we laughed. "Whoa." Both of my hands came to his cheeks, and I held him back. "Have you been practicing?"

A smirk crept onto his face. "I've daydreamed about doing that for a long time."

I blushed, blinking, and tried to remember why I tapped the brakes.

"You're chill? Are we good? I know we didn't finish our conversation yesterday," I said, savoring his minty smell.

"How about we enjoy this?" His hands found mine. "We can worry about the consequences when we're dead." He snorted.

"That's not funny."

"No?" He pulled me against his chest. "I can do this all day."

"Daniel." Mrs. Eppstein's voice sounded from the kitchen. Daniel and I jumped away from each other. I patted my hair as I sat next to my backpack, and he wiped his mouth with his sleeve.

"Daniel?" She walked into the living room and paused, her eyes narrowing. "Oh Maya, you're here."

My body froze as I searched my mind for a response.

"Yes, we are going on another drive today," Daniel said, his thumbs hooking into the belt loops of his jeans.

"Oh." Another pause. "I see." She takes a deep breath. "You're not doing too much, are you?"

Daniel and I both shook our heads, and I sealed my lips, doing my best not to give myself away. I looked down at my backpack to hide my face. "But before we go, Daniel, I have those books you loaned me." Mrs. Eppstein's heels clicked as she returned to the kitchen.

"You finished them?" Daniel asked too loud, his eyes on the place where his mother stood seconds before.

My zipper screamed as I opened my backpack. The items inside announced their existence with loud rustling, my nerves buzzed with each sound. I frowned as I pulled the novels out.

He took them, looking at the covers as if he'd never seen them before. Then, without a word, he walked to the kitchen. The lyrical sound of Yiddish, with its hushes and brisk silences, traveled to me from the other room. Uncomfortable, I started organizing my backpack, ignoring what sounded like an intimate conversation. The papers I stacked curled in the corners from the sweat on my palms.

"Maya."

I looked up as the door shut. Daniel held his books to his chest, and his face bore the red splotches he often donned in my presence. He shook his head as if to answer the question that brought my brows reaching for my hairline.

"Does she know?"

He continued to shake his head. "No. She wants me to stay home today." He sat next to me. "She's worried I'm doing too much too soon."

"She's probably right." I blew out a breath. "Should I go?"

"Stay. She forgot her lunch. She's heading back to work now." He stretched out sideways, resting his head in my lap and hanging his legs off the divan arm. "What if I picked another book, and you read it to me?"

I pushed a spiral of his hair off his forehead. "We could, or we could do more of this." I curled around him, pressing my lips to his.

DAY 753

12/12/1983

The week before Christmas, I found myself consumed by the secret world Daniel and I created for ourselves. In this world, he became healthy, and I became single. Outside the warmth of our bubble, I picked fights with Rob. His beatings became my repentance for my unfaithfulness. My mouth filled with ash and rage in his presence. Letting those angry words fly before seeing my angel cleansed my soul. I wanted to be the girl Daniel saw when he looked at me.

Today, I existed in my Daniel vacuum. We drove, the heater up high, the music up high, my mood up high. The happiness energized me, sending my toes tapping and my cheeks quivering from a compulsory smile. It made me want more, and it made me want it now.

"Wait, pull in there." I pointed to a parking lot ahead of us.

Daniel raised his brows but followed my direction, turning on his blinker. He took a right at the slowest possible speed, and a car behind us honked, speeding past as the driver raised a frustrated hand. "Should I park?" Unfazed, Daniel leaned forward as he peered over the dashboard at the empty lot and the motel on the other side. The tan building used orange doors and curtains to break up its blandness.

"Just pull into that spot." I pointed next to the office. My palms dampened as the car halted, my resolve wavering. My fingers fumbled as I unbuckled my seatbelt. "I'll be right back." I pushed the door open against the cold and hopped out of the car before Daniel, or my conscience could protest.

Ten minutes later, I knocked on his window, dangling a key between my fingers. His knuckles whitened as he gripped the steering wheel. I pulled his door open, breaking his trance. "What's going on?" A trace of a smile lined his lip as he worried it with his teeth.

"You'll see." With hungry eyes, I watched his slim form unfold from the car. He followed me to room eight, where I turned on the lights and closed the window shades.

Daniel stood by the door, his fingers still on the lock, wide-eyed. He coughed. "*Ketsele*, I—"

"One minute." I dug in my purse, past the foil packets I'd tossed in there the other day and to the marker I use at work.

"What are you doing?" His hands had found each other in their usual way as he waited.

"It's a tradition I wanted to start." I went to the side table and, getting down on my knees, wrote on the underside.

"What's it say?"

I smirked. "*Daniel was here.*"

He barks a laugh, his shoulders relaxing. "Well, that's a weird reason to get a room at a place like this."

I walked up to him. "You know why I got a room at a place like this."

"Do I?" He looks at the bed.

"Life is too short to wait." My hands found his hips, allowing myself to live in the moment. "I want you."

He pulled me to his chest. "*Ketsele*," he said into my hair. Our eyes met, and then our lips.

We did the clumsy walk lovers do.

Each backward step a near-fall.

We took turns leaning, as we stumbled, driven by tangled limbs.

We moved together to the rhythm of skipped heartbeats.

Seconds and hours lived inside of us as we struggled with buttons and shoelaces, our hearts and minds consumed by lust.

His hand lifted the hem of my shirt and dragged it over my head.

Daniel gasped.

Silence.

The moment fractured like ice under pressure.

He held me at arm's length.

I struggled to slow my panting as I registered his tension.

His face contorted in a strange mix of anguish and fear.

My hands came up to cover my naked skin.

He reached out and traced a dark blue line marking my torso. I watched his eyes bounce from the handprints circling each of my biceps and the splotches of bruising across my rib cage. The injuries spanned the spectrum between green and purple, bearing testament to the violence at home.

His finger lifted to a yellowing shadow below my collarbone. "You promised." He whispered to the mar on my skin, running his thumb along it as if to rub it away.

I opened my mouth, remembering that day at the bus stop and how I would have said anything to make his sadness go away.

He pulled my body against his and rested his head on my shoulder. His tears pressed into my neck. He grunted as he lifted me, and though he struggled I let him deposit me on the bed. I looked away as his lung caught up with his actions. His ragged breaths filling me with shame and a shutter.

Finally, he knelt beside me, one of his hands finding mine. His eyes returned to my torso. One at a time, he pressed his lips to my injuries. His kisses outlined Rob's sins, highlighting the promise I made with no intentions of keeping.

My fingers curled into his hair when he rested his head on my stomach. "I'm going to kill him." He covered his face with his hands.

"Daniel, he's not an evil man—"

"Feh!" His voice thickened with the first hint of anger I've heard from him. "He is the evilest man I've met." His hands cut the space above him; his nostrils flared as he took three deep breaths.

One, in and out. His chest rose and fell.

Two, in and out. His hands found each other, his fingers interlocking.

Three, in and out. His jaw loosened, his lashes fluttered.

His face relaxed as he lie next to me, staring up unblinking.

"I'm sorry."

"Don't apologize for what he does to you. It's not your fault."

I sat up to retrieve my shirt.

His hand shot out and rested on my back.

"But it is." I shook my head as I reached over him. "I didn't think this through." I pulled my shirt back on with jerky movements and then used the scrunchy around my wrist to tie my hair away from my face.

Daniel found my hand, and I squeezed it, thinking of the unopened condom in my purse.

"You don't deserve to be hurt."

I turned away from him. "I ask for it, Daniel."

"No one. Should. Ever. Hurt you." The blanket of silence suffocated me.

"We should go."

"What if you married me?" he said as I spoke.

"Wait, what?" I looked down. The cleft in his chin jutted out, his thick brows becoming set and serious as our eyes met.

"If you married me, you could get away from him, and when I die, I will leave you the car and my college savings. You could start fresh."

"First off, it's called a 'college savings' for a reason." I closed my eyes contemplating a world without Daniel in it. "Secondly and most importantly you're not going to die." I willed my words to be true with every part of my soul.

"*Ketsele,* I'm going to die. I want to take care of you when I'm gone. I don't want to leave knowing you are still living with that monster."

I pushed his hand away. "It's not your job to take care of me."

He mumbled something as I scooted to the edge of the bed.

"What did you say?"

"You're not taking care of yourself." His voice came

hard, hitting me in the gut. "You're not taking care of yourself and we all know I'm not going to live long enough to go college."

"How would you know?" My fear brought me to my feet, tears burning my eyes.

"I wouldn't know. I'm a child to you." He sat crossed-legged, his back against the headboard.

"You are a kid."

"And so are you."

"No. I never was."

"This is ridiculous. Why are we fighting about this? He hurts you." His hands gesture to me, as his voice became gentle. "You should leave him."

"You don't get it."

He held his breath, his eyes closing and I watched his body transform. His muscles loosened, his face relaxed. "Maya, come here."

His eyes and arms and heart opened before my eyes. I wished I could find the right words to explain myself. I followed his lead, filling my chest with air, doing my best to speak calmly. "Here's the thing about Rob. He brought me to Philly. He kept me safe. I'm all he has and he is all I have." I sat back down, my eyes meeting his. "He's the only one who really knows me."

"I know you, *ketsele*. I see you in the hero of every book I read and feel you in every breath I take." He opened his hands to me. "Come here. So I can hold you and get to know you better."

I settled in his arms. "I'm not a hero."

"You saved me." He stroked my cheek and I wondered what he needed saving from.

I curled into him and time rolled past us as we sat in our own heads. Together, but apart.

"Let's take Rob's power away."

"What?" I didn't want Rob's name in his mouth. It felt dirty and wrong.

"I can be someone who 'really knows you.'" He kissed my forehead. "I can be someone who 'has you', you can be someone who 'has me.'"

I nodded, as I processed the logic of what he said. Even if it made sense, I lacked the courage to put to words the images flashing in my head.

"What if I start? It can be a confession for a confession." He smoothed my hair and waited for a response.

"Okay."

"Some days I can't get out of bed—" His Adam's apple Jedbed as he swallowed. "My dad carries me from room to room." He kissed me, stroking my arm as he waited. "Your turn."

I closed my eyes. "We were homeless for years." My throat burned, my vocal cords on fire as if to trap my words inside. For a short time, I became lost in silence.

"I take eight pills every morning so I can eat." His voice broke through the hurt, becoming my touchstone.

I licked my lips. "I've stolen from people who have tried to help me." I matched my breathing to his.

"I know my parents purchased a headstone and a burial plot for me. Sometimes, I think it will be easier on them when I'm gone."

My eyes opened, finding a brown spot on the ceiling. It swam on the other side of my unshed tears. A sight I've seen in other hotel rooms. "We sold our bodies." My voice cracked, and I curled into Daniel. A moan escaped my lips, and he held me against his chest as if my grief would carry me away if he didn't tether me down. And maybe it would.

I let the rocking of his chest and his gentle hands soothe me as I mourned our lost childhoods—Rob's, mine, Daniel's.

Three sharp knocks sounded from across the room. Startled, I sat straight up, wiping at my face.

"Fifteen minutes!" A man's shout traveled through the door.

Our eyes met. "Thank you for trusting me," he said, a sad smile on his face. "You are so strong."

DAY 752

12/13/1983

"I want to go on a date."

I paused my dusting, not sure if I'd heard him speak or imagined it.

"I don't want to feel like we are sneaking around." He sat on the couch next to the bookshelf where I dusted. "I want to take you out and spoil you. Like a boyfriend would." He crossed his legs and looked up at me.

"Like a boyfriend, huh?" I asked, replacing a book and pulling out another.

"Yes, because that's what you deserve."

"Hmm?" I didn't look at him, but a wall of his eagerness pressed against my side. "It sounds like you already have a plan."

He stood, stepping behind me and wrapping his arms around my waist. "I do. It's the perfect plan, so you can't say no."

I smiled, leaning into him. "Tell me more."

"It's complicated."

"You know me. 'Complicated' is my middle name."

DAY 741

12/24/1983

"I'll be staying late to help clean up, so don't wait up for me." I leaned forward and applied my fourth layer of mascara, a cloud of Aquanet stinging my eyes.

Rob stood in the bathroom doorway, nursing a beer. "Don't they know it's a holiday?" His eyes met mine through the glass.

"It's a Christmas Eve party, Rob." Or that's what I told him every time he asked. There would be no party. Each time I spoke the lie, the deception became easier.

I got home from the diner early, showered, teased my hair, and slid on the only dress I owned. Even with its simple A-line cut and midnight blue color, I felt beautiful. My matching eyeshadow brought my skin tone to a glow as it shimmered. I couldn't wait to show Daniel my transformation. Rob caught my eye as I smiled. It fell from my face.

"You're going to your cousins, aren't you?" I clipped on my earrings, trying to keep my hands steady.

"Yeah, but I miss *you*."

I slipped past him into our bedroom and shut the door between us—stockings and heels, ready to go.

I entered the hall where Rob leaned against the wall, waiting for me. "You're looking sexy."

I folded my arms. "Thanks." I held my breath as he studied me and took a step in my direction.

His hands came to my waist, his head lowering to my shoulder. "Babe, can't you stay longer?" His husky voice tickled my ear where his lips touched.

"I can't, running late." I tried to straighten my elbows, my arms meaning to pry us apart. He held me tighter.

"But Baby, it's been so long." He kissed my neck, and my throat worked as I tried not to gag.

I squirmed, repulsion crawling under my skin. "Rob, stop." I tilted my chin back, dodging his mouth as it came to mine.

He squeezed the breath out of me, and giving up on a kiss, he sucked hard at my neck.

Unable to breathe, my limbs took over, my muscles tightening against him as I struggled. Finally, I stomped my heel into his foot, and he growled as his grip loosened.

"You bitch." He shoved me against the wall, forcing his knee between my legs. "What? You think you're too good for me?" He wrapped his fingers in my hair and mashed his mouth against mine.

I grit my teeth against the taste of beer and cigarettes.

He pulled back, his brows knitting together, his mouth glittering with spit.

"I hate you." I shouldn't have said it. The defeated look on his face of frowning eyes and lifting lower lip became a snarl.

His palm met my forehead with such force my neck stretched as my head slammed against the wall. At first, blackness filled my vision, then white spots. In the seconds it took for me to see again, Rob's finger climbed up my dress, ripping my stockings and fumbling with my panties. Under the layers of ringing in my ears, I could hear his voice. Though I couldn't recognize the words.

I hit and kicked and pulled at the skirt of my dress to cover the target of his heavy hands. When my feet left the ground I cried out and I plunged down the stairs, I couldn't tell if I fell or he sent me flying.

Bounce.

Crack.

Shoulder. Back.

Thump, thump, thump.

Landing with the taste of blood.

My toes moved. My fingers did too. But the rest of my joints locked themselves into place and refused to aid in my escape. Pain baptized me, taking my breath away.

The sound of his bare feet as they slapped against the wood of each step sent my eyes wild. "Maya, oh Maya." He dropped to the floor and scooped me up, tears reddening his eyes. "Look what you've done to yourself."

I struggled to shape words with my sore jaw, the shock of the fall melting away with renewed fear as, once again, he held me. "Let me go," I said, and I meant it in more ways than one. My weak movements did not garner a response from him.

"You can't go now. You're a mess." He pressed the corner of his shirt against my bloody nose.

I pushed his hand away. "You can't keep me here."

His eyes darkened as with a heave, he lifted me, carrying me to the coat closet. He tossed me in. I landed on my side as he slammed the door closed behind me.

The blackness ate my screams and tears, and I came to

my knees to bang on the door, noticing a slight give with each blow as Rob held it closed. "Please, let me out! Please!"

When my aches caught up to me, I slid to the ground. My hands traced my body, testing one injury at a time. I probed the wetness of my hair, wincing as I did, then removed my single remaining earring and dropped it on the ground. *Can I run?* I climbed to my feet, lifting one leg and then the other, and hunted in the dark for my coat and my shoes, my mind on the angel who waited for me.

The doorbell rang, and my hand found the knob. Rob didn't move. After a pause, it rang again. Rob shifted, and the floorboards creaked. A few more heartbeats and my doorbell went nutso.

Ding.

Ding.

Di–ng-dong. Ding-dong. D–i–ng.

I heard hinges rattle as Rob's weight lifted and his footfalls sounded.

"Who is it?"

I pushed the closet open and bolted, running straight for the back door. Out of the corner of my eye, Daniel stood in a suit, standing at the front door, his hands squeezed into fists at his side. His eyes followed my path.

I found my way to the bus stop half-blind and crumpled on the bench, my legs curled up against my body, my face pressed into my knees.

"Maya?" Daniel's soft voice sounded distant. "Maya, let me take you home. I'm worried Rob will come looking for you. He seemed drunk, he was surprised to see me." His hand rested on my shoulder.

My body jerked away of its own volition, and he took a step back. "Don't touch me." My hands came to my head, shaking as they tried to hold it together. "It hurts so much." I bit my coat sleeve and moaned. "I can't move."

He draped his jacket over me, sitting next to me. A song replaced the silence of night.

"*Shlof mayn kind.*" His baritone stretched the throaty vowels of his Yiddish into a lullaby. His coughs broke up the verses, reminding me of the last time I sang to him. "*Shlof zhe, zunenyu.*"

His song finished. "Maya, can we try to go in?" He cleared his throat and took a quick breath. "I'm having a hard time catching my breath." Shame dripped from his words.

I nodded, my brain bouncing around in my skull. I uncurled myself, touching each foot to the ground, the painstaking process intermittently halted by the ache in my ribs. I took Daniel's arm, and we made the journey from the bus stop to his living room.

In the lighted living room, I could see the runs in my stockings, the rips in my dress, the blood. "I planned on looking pretty for you tonight, but now I must look hella punk." I probed my nose.

"You need a shower." He answered, his face a calculating mask as he studied me.

"What? Am I underdressed?" I leaned against the wall, wishing to lie on the ground. "Remind me. Your parents won't be home until tomorrow?"

He nodded. "Maya, I should take you to the hospital." He lifted his hand to the lapel of my coat. "Let me help you—"

"Don't touch me." I hugged myself, my skin crawling in the place where he touched.

His hand shot back to his side, his body stiffening. "I'm sorry." He stepped back.

How is it that I want him to hold me and am disgusted about the idea all at the same time? "No, I'm sorry. I'm not angry at you. I'm embarrassed, I—" my thoughts drifted off to the moment when I saw him on the other side of the door. *I am angry at him.* "I mean, what were you thinking?"

He tilted his head, his eyes round with surprise. "You mean coming over tonight?"

"He could have hurt you."

He nodded his head. "He could have."

"And you think I'd be okay with that?"

"No, but I'd be more upset with myself if I didn't go and you got hurt even worse." He rubbed his chest, lines forming on his face that would never become permanent. "Can this be the end of it?"

"The end of what?" My raw throat stuck to the words. *Did he want to say goodbye? Was he done with me?*

"To you and Rob."

A fresh set of tears filled my eyes as I nodded my answer. He opened his arms, and I went to him.

DAY 740

12/25/1983

On Christmas morning, I woke to the sound of a gurgling engine. My head gained ten pounds overnight, and the sound reverberated in my eardrums like bees. My eyes fluttered open with difficulty. The wall of books reminded me I slept in Daniel's bed last night, a towel over his mother's cotton sham, our fingers laced together most of the night. I turned back to the pillow and breathed in his minty scent.

I turned back to Daniel, where he sat cross-legged in the middle of his bed. A book sat open in front of him—a strange pipe thing in his mouth. The plastic mouthpiece emitted a stream of mist from the opposite end. The room smelled of chemicals and Vicks.

He waved and placed a bookmark on the page he read. He looked at his watch and pulled the piece from his mouth. "I have two minutes. Can you wait?"

I nodded, and he returned to breathing in his medicine, but not before extending his hand to me. I took it, studying his face, then the machine, and then his fingers. I rubbed my thumb over each fingernail, feeling the width of his fingertips. For the first time, I noticed the thickness matched the thickness of his knuckles. Daniel turned off the machine. "It's called clubbing." He took his hand back. "The way my fingertips are bigger, it happens over time with decreased oxygenation." He set the tubing aside and scooted up the bed until he sat next to me.

He opened his mouth and then held up his finger as he coughed into his shoulder. He jumped off the bed and grabbed a tissue from his dresser, spitting into it. "Sorry. That always happens after–" He coughed twice more and slumped into the bed. "How are you?"

"Confused." I took a deep breath. "And relieved, and my body hurts." I forced a smile and touched the back of my head with a wince. "I must look like hell."

"I want to help you get cleaned up." He watched me, thinking for several minutes before pushing on. "Do you want to talk about it? What happened?"

I swallowed hard and looked into his eyes, his warm and honest eyes. "Can you hold me?" He came to me and opened his arms, waiting for me to find my place. I climbed into his lap and buried my face in his neck while avoiding any contact with my nose. "He—" I breathed in deep, trying to stay chill, "he tried—"

I wrapped my arms around Daniel, and his hands settled on my back. "I'm sorry. I ruined everything, but I couldn't let him." My voice became an unrecognizable whine as I forced out the words I wouldn't have said to anyone else. "I'm not his anymore."

"You're not anyone's, Maya." He leaned forward and kissed my hair. "You are yours and no one else's."

I nodded my head and sniffled and stole his strength.

We sat there until light crept into the sky beyond his second-floor window.

"Okay." He patted my back. "Let's get you cleaned up before my parents get home?" He posed his statement as a question, and though I'd rather not move again for days, I conceded. He picked out a t-shirt and some flannel pajama pants from his drawer before leading me to the bathroom. After putting the toilet lid down, he settled me there as he ran a bath.

He undressed me, and I imagined he'd experienced this treatment many times in his life. I stepped into the water and grieved for Daniel, his first time seeing a naked woman would be clinical and cloaked in sadness. I used my arms and hands to maintain a semblance of modesty as I looked away from him.

The water stung my knees, a few spots on my right shin, and my palms. Daniel filled a cup with water, and I leaned forward. I watched mesmerized as the water turned a deeper shade of pink with every rinse of my hair. Then Daniel dabbed at my cut with a washcloth.

Once he freed my hair, I fell back into the warmth, my breasts floating to the top of the water. A blush rose in Daniel's cheeks. Remembering myself, my arms folding, my knee coming up to hide the rest of my body.

He looked away as he dipped his rag back into the bath. "Let me clean up your face , and I'll leave you to yourself," he said, a new shyness keeping his eyes averted. He dabbed at my face, sucking at his teeth every time I flinched away.

When he left, I considered sinking underneath the water and never returning to the surface for air. But the Eppsteins gave me a reason to breathe—all of them, including the dad who I'd yet to meet. I couldn't mar the beautiful life they built with a few minutes of my selfishness.

I dried off before pulling the plug and sat wrapped in a towel, watching as parts of me went down the drain. I mourned as if attending a funeral. The ones you go to because you are obligated—the ones where the world is better off now they're gone. I watched traces of my blood and strands of my hair whorl in circles around the drain before disappearing, *good riddance.*

Goodbye, Rob.

Goodbye, child Maya.

Goodbye.

We sat at the dining table eating cereal when the Eppsteins walked in. The smiles slid from their faces as their eyes landed on me.

Daniel stood. "Mom." She held up her hand, and his mouth snapped shut.

"Maya, what happened?" She asked.

"My boyfriend pushed me down the stairs." My eyes burn with shame and an ache building behind my eyes. "I didn't have anywhere else to go."

"And so she's here?" She turned to Daniel, her arms pinned to her sides. Her continued stiffness surprised me.

"*Mamala,* it was the right thing to do." Daniel always sounded younger when he spoke to his mother.

Mr. Eppstein stepped forward. "It was right to have a woman sleep over while your parents weren't home?"

Daniel flopped back into his chair, his arms folded over his chest.

Mr. Eppstein folded his arms with the same look on his

face. This is what Daniel would look like if he grew up. "Mr. and Mrs. Eppstein," I said, standing and swaying as dizziness overtook me. "I'll go." The cloud of ringing returned to my ears stole my resolve.

Mrs. Eppstein looked me up and down. "Dressed in that?" She turned to Daniel. "In my son's clothes."

"He ruined my dress, I don't—" my fist came to my forehead; talking made the ache worse.

"Sit back down." I caught my breath at her interruption and did as told. Her heels sounded as she circled the table. I turned to her as she came to stand in front of me, and she tipped my chin up. Her eyes scanned my face. "Are you hurt anywhere else?"

"The back of her head," Daniel spoke between bites. He returned to his cereal as if the confrontation had never happened. Mr. Eppstein settled into the chair next to Daniel, picking up the cereal box to study the text on the back. Mrs. Eppstein's sudden interest in my injuries gave the men silent permission to return to normal.

"Ouch." She cringed as she parted the hair on the back of my head. "I need to tape it closed." She turned to her husband. "What do you think, Aaron? Should we call the police?"

"No."

Mrs. Eppstein's hands weighed my shoulders down as I slid to the edge of my chair, the blood draining from my face. I gripped the sides of the table as I considered running.

"Let the adults talk." She sat next to me, her hand covering mine. "We can help, *Shiksa*."

I jumped when Daniel's fists landed on the table. Her smile dropped as she turned to him. "So what?" He stood. "You think of her as a *Goy*, but—" The following Yiddish made both of his parents flinch.

"You don't mean that." Mrs. Eppstein frowned, her hand pulling back from mine as if it would poison her.

Daniel turned to his father. "You agree. I know you do."

The parents looked at each other. They didn't share a word. Mr. Eppstein's raised brows mirrored his wife's, and her frown reflected his. This new silent contention confused me.

Daniel stood and extended his hand. I took it and followed him up the stairs.

"Are they mad at me?" I'd never had parents to argue over me before. *What was I supposed to do?*

"No, they're mad at me." He went to his dresser and started opening pill bottles.

"Why did you decide to tell them?"

"My mother called you a gentile." He shook his head. He popped a handful of pills in his mouth and gulped the water he'd brought with him. "But it's worse than that. It's more like she's calling you a temptress. I think she suspected we were together. She was trying to goad me."

"Well, it worked."

Stepping in front of me, he kissed my cheek. "You should stay with me." He kissed my other cheek.

"What about your parents?"

"I told them God gave me a short time on this earth, and I would take whatever love he provided me." He kissed my forehead. "You look tired. Take a nap. I'll go down to start the negotiations with my parents."

The door clicks closed behind him.

I curled up beside the book he'd left sitting on the bed; *The Color Purple*. I recognized the title as one he wanted to share with me. I rested my hand on the cover, the mauve of the title matching the bruise wrapped around my wrist. I closed my eyes to the sight, the pounding in my head not allowing anymore tears.

I WOKE to the sound of the bedroom door opening. Pale faced Mrs. Eppstein stepped inside, her dainty fingers finding the light switch. "We'd like you to come downstairs so we can talk."

I sat up and rubbed my eyes. "Where's Daniel?"

"We asked him to visit with his grandparents while the adults figured this out." Her icy voice replaced her usual kindness.

Daniel left me?

Sweeping my hair back over my shoulders, I followed her from the room and down the stairs. The swelling around my eye had worsened while I slept, making my vision narrow. I froze when I saw who sat on the couch next to Mr. Eppstein.

"Maya." Rob came to me in two strides. "I was so worried about you."

I held my breath.

"I called that emergency contact number you gave me, thinking I'd get a hold of your mom or your dad. Rob answered." Mrs. Eppstein went to her husband's side.

"And after I told Mrs. Eppstein about the accident, she asked me to come over. It sounds like you don't remember what happened last night." Rob held me by the shoulders and leaned forward to see my face better. He touched my nose, and I flinched away. "You must have hit your head hard, babe."

Rob wrapped his arm around my waist. The two Eppsteins stood opposite, their tight faces relaxing as Rob spoke. I froze. Every part of me turned solid. My brain and body divorced each other as I floated in a flat despair. Like a dream, I listened to Rob's honeyed words, and then, with his hand around my wrist, I followed him home.

I went straight upstairs and to our bedroom, locking the door, and falling onto the bed; my brain abuzz, my body numb.

"Don't have a cow, Maya." He spoke from the door. "We've had worse fights."

"You could have killed me."

"You legit threw yourself down the stairs on your own."

"Robert, did you hear me? I could have died."

"No shit, Sherlock." I jumped at the sound of him rattling the doorknob. "Let me in." He shook it again. "It was a major accident, and I'm sorry. I'll be a better man for you."

"Tough." I pulled the covers over my head. "You can be a better man for someone else." I closed my eyes. "I'm done. I've been done for a long time."

"Maya." My name became a plea on his lips. "I love you."

I swallowed. "I love you too, but I'm not yours anymore."

Through the blanket and the door, I could feel him standing there, his hands pressing on the wood. My heart ached because his heart ached and I hated it.

I pushed my fists to my chest, letting them rock with my breaths. I thought of my angel and how he left me. *You are yours and no one else's*. I knew he'd come for me.

DAY 621

4/21/84

Rob and I created a new and proper waltz out of our daily lives. The room became mine. I kept the door locked at all times and did my best not to wander from it unless I was leaving the house. He kept his hands to himself, though his knuckles often whitened when we happened upon each other, his eyes following me as I made my escapes.

Losing my second job meant my dream of having my apartment would take longer than expected, but instead of working those hours, I found myself at the library studying for my GED. Daniel, insatiable Daniel, inspired me to reach further than I thought possible. I would not work at the diner for the rest of my life.

Though he became my reason for waking in the morning, I tried not to think of him. My heart broke so hard I still found splinters littered in those times requiring vulnerability. Whenever my breaths lost their rhythm, I'd close my eyes and conjure visions of him in a suit, his hand on the doorbell. Whenever a book's sad story brought me to tears, I'd feel the ghost of his arms holding me; and on those early mornings I spent at our bus stop, I'd look up at his window and feel warmth.

Months crawled by, and I read every book Daniel mentioned to me. As fifth in line at the library for *The Color Purple*, I waited longer for the book than any other but, in the end, took the least amount of time to read it. The novel haunted me for days. It's concepts fluttered across my mind at random. I thought about how Celie redefined God as an It, and how if I were to believe in a God I would feel the same. Imagining a genderless, formless higher power all around us comforted me. These thoughts reminded me of Mrs and Mr Epsteins' God.

Would their God have sent me away in my time of need? Was it my godlessness or my skin color that made me not good enough for their son?

But the thought that lingered between my ears returned me to Daniel. *Did he hand me the book with Celie in mind? Did he see the abuse she suffered from her step-father and her husband and think of me? Am I a broken thing?*

The ending, oh the ending.

Torn in two, I closed the book with angry tears in my eyes. Part of me wanted to curl on the ground and pretend I had a sister to hold. The other part of me wanted to toss the book into the toilet. How dare Walker diminish the struggle with a perfect reunion? Those tears couldn't erase the pain. Those hugs never would've happened in real life. In real life, Albert would have beat Celie to death, and Nettie would have drowned in the ocean. That's how life worked. There is no washing your past down the drain and walking away.

DAY 614

4/28/1984

"Take a chill pill, Jed. I'll be right there." I walked around the counter, coffee pot in hand.

"Thanks, brat," he said as I poured.

"You're welcome, old man." The nutty aroma filled the air and he winked at me.

The bells on the door jingled, and I turned to greet the new customer.

My angel stood there with a grin on his face. Daniel looked taller and thinner than I remembered.

The coffee pot found its way to Jed's table, and I ran. Not trusting my eyes, I needed to touch him. Daniel caught me, his arms pulled me against his bony chest, and my hands wandered his body in disbelief.

"Ketsele."

"Where have you been?" I asked as he wiped the tears from my eyes.

"Connecticut." He groaned as he found my face with his hands. "I'm so sorry." His lips parted and his eyes squeezed shut. "I'm so gullible and dependent and shouldn't have ever left your side."

I pulled him to an empty booth and sat down beside him. "I don't know what to say." I leaned against him, taking his hand.

"Don't say anything. Come with me on an adventure. We can talk on the way."

"Go with you? When?" I sat up, my skin crawling as my body remembered the sadness of the last few months.

"Now." He looked around at the two customers who sat at their tables in silence. "Let's go now." His energy sobered, his hand loosening, but the twinkle in his eyes remained.

"Go where?"

"Anywhere!" He cleared his throat and lowered his voice. "I want to see Niagara Falls and the Capital." His eyes locked with mine. "If you came with me to see the biggest ball of yarn, I'd be happy."

"And what will we do when you run out of medication? How will we pay for this?" I pulled my hand away and shook my head. "I've had more days without you than I had with you, Daniel. Do you understand what you're asking me to do?" I sighed. "It's not right."

"'I far rather be happy than right any day.'" He smirked as he quoted Hitchhiker's Guide.

I rolled my eyes as he poked his elbow at me.

"'Don't panic'?" His grin returned.

I did my best not to smile. "I still can't believe you made me read that book."

"You loved it."

"I hated every second, it was the mostar ridiculous thing I've ever read. It drove me crazy."

"And you endured it for me?"

I blew out a breath. "Daniel."

"Do this for me."

"Daniel."

"*Ketsele.*"

"Daniel."

"Don't make me remind you. I can die at any minute." He smiled.

"That's not funny." I smacked my hand on the table. "You've been gone for months." I rubbed my face with both of my hands. "Months. I never thought I'd see you again. What if I moved on?"

"You didn't greet me like you've moved on."

"And what about your parents?"

"Maya, right now, all I need is you." He kissed my cheek and then my lips.

I breathed him in. I should have hesitated—I should have said "no," but I missed him too much.

I opened my mouth.

I opened my mouth and let his tongue in.

The bell on the door jingled, and I pulled myself away from Daniel.

"Keep the change," said Jed. By the time I turned, the door had swished closed.

"That was not the kiss of a girl who's moved on." Daniel wrapped his arm around my shoulder. "Tell me, what's keeping you here?"

I thought of Rob and this job. I thought of my daily ritual of checking the mail for my GED exam results and my savings hidden in a tin behind the flour at home and the library book sitting on my dresser. I looked at Daniel, my heart skipped a beat, and I decided. "Okay."

"Okay?" His shoulders pulled back and his chin tucked in.

"Okay, but I need to finish this shift. And then I need to get some of my–"

He pulled me into a kiss, and I relaxed against him.

When the bells interrupted us for the second time, I rested my hand on his chest, holding him back. "Oh, and I have to do this." I pulled the marker from my pocket and, leaning over the corner of the table, wrote, *DANIEL WAS HERE.*

He watched over my shoulder, his laughter filling my chest with wonder.

DAY 61

11/2/1984

Catherine,

Little one, I wanted to start this letter by sharing a quote from The Great Midash: G-d takes nothing from the world until he puts something else in its place. I don't want you to feel like it's your job to replace me. What I want you to get out of this quote is that you are a blessing. In my opinion the best blessing to have ever walked this earth.

I just made your mother promise your name would be Catherine if you came out a girl. What she doesn't know is you are definitely a girl. That made it very simple for me to agree to her silly wish to name you Daniel junior if you're a boy. Cat, your mother doesn't know that you are a junior in your own way. I've always called your mother Ketsele, which is Yiddish for kitten, little kitten.

Cat, I'm writing to you because it's looking like I won't be around when you're born. I'm sorry about that. I'm sorry that I didn't get to know you. I wish I could have stayed longer. Know that I wanted you with all my heart and plan to watch you from the afterlife. When I finally see you in person, I hope to see your mother on your face. There is not a more beautiful woman. But, for now, all I can do is give you my story.

I was born on February 29th, 1964, a leap year baby. My actual last birthday happened the year after I met your mother. She constantly reminded me how young I was. Little did she know I'd had a lot fewer birthdays than she assumed. My luck was this kind of luck. I was born with a genetic disease to the best parents possible. I was born on a day that occurs every four years to a family that would celebrate on both February 28th and March 1st. G-d gave me a brief life, with a chance to meet your mother.

My parents found out about my Cystic Fibrosis the day after I was born. I had a condition called meconium ileus. This condition only occurs in infants with CF. I immediately went to surgery. My mother prayed. My father researched. When I returned to them, they made a promise. They vowed to my infant self they would never teach me to fear death.

They wanted me to love the life I had. And I did. I read every book that interested me. I explored my religion and my culture. I lived longer than we ever thought I could, and they did everything possible to make my time happy.

I'm sure your mother told you how we found each other by now, how we met at a bus stop in the middle of the night. What she couldn't tell you is that I fell in love when I first saw her through my bedroom window. I can blame Zorro, Robin Hood, and Wesley. They taught me how to fall for the damsel in distress. Your mother and I took turns being the hero. The strength that peeked out from under her rough edges was the first thing to attract me to her.

We didn't have an easy start. Your mom and I shouldn't have happened. Ask Mary and Aaron Eppstein. They did their best to keep us apart after I admitted my feelings. That day they sent me to my grandparents' house to talk to your mother in private. I sat at their kitchen table, waiting to be called home. I sat there late into the night, ignoring the invitation to eat dinner or relax in the living room.

Dad came to pick me up at 11:00 pm. I got into the car, and he told me that your mother had gone home with Rob. I didn't believe it. I couldn't believe it. I was already planning to go straight to her house when we got home. We never went home.

We drove most of the night. I was livid.

He'd betrayed me, the one person who I thought would be on my side. He talked and talked.

He tried to explain away the treachery. He tried to blame my mother. He tried to blame our religion, but he was the one driving the car. I vomited twice on the way there. The farther Maya was from me, the more it tore me apart. They tried taking your mother away from me. It was the darkest time of my life. He left me at my aunt's house in Connecticut. This was my mother's sister, and she was far more Jewish than I'd been raised. I think my parents hoped she could dissuade me from my infatuation with a Goy.

I don't want you to hate my parents. I don't. I've forgiven them. I hope they have forgiven me. I couldn't be the good Jewish boy they wanted me to be. I'm okay with that, and I think G-d is okay with it too. I think he planned to take their son, so he gave them a daughter.

I spent those four months trying to escape. Made it back to PA even. Ended up at a hospital for seven days before being sent back. It wasn't until the end of my time with them I realized all I needed to do was lie. So that's what I did. I told them what they wanted to hear. That I was over your mother. That I saw the errors in my ways and just wanted to go home so I could finish school. Soon enough, my aunt did just that. She sent me home. Home to save my girl.

The first day they left me alone, I went to her, sat in the diner with her and apologized. I saw the hurt in her face, and I hated myself for it. Hated *myself for my age. Hated myself for my sickness. Little girl, I've never been the self-loathing type. I hope you never are, but if you ever find that in yourself, look at your mother. She banished my hate. She can banish yours. She's magic like that.*

I think we argued. I may have cried. Your father is a crier. Eventually, that thing between us won out. It won out over the fear and the inbred tabooness. I took her hand and walked away from that place. There was a smile on her face. A smile I recognized, and I knew we were back in December again, back in that moment when we were our closest, when we were both free.

I have to tell you something about your mother. You may already know this, but she is an absolute pessimist. Even as we drove away, I saw the doubt on her face. I imagined her pinching herself, trying to wake herself from our dream. It was a little scary, the risk. We had nothing but the car, Maya's savings, a pile of books, and a month of my medications.

I drove until I had to stop to do my nebulizer. We grabbed a hotel and Maya went to get food. When she got back, I taught her how to do my physiotherapy. It was strange doing my CF ritual with her, but your mother's a natural. I like to imagine that she'll go to school and become a nurse when I'm gone.

We saw Niagara Falls, the Empire State Building, and the Statue of Liberty. Rob had been

Maya's prison; and mine—mine was this body. Maya took me places I would have never gone without her.

After a few weeks on the road, we found a church. It is funny that we had a Christian wedding when neither of us was that religious. But, it felt right—right to have G-d there, even if it wasn't the one that I'd prayed to all my life.

I called home when I ran out of medications. Baby girl, if you ever leave your mother, please make sure you call home sooner than I did. We break our parents' hearts. That's what kids do. Try to keep it to a minimum. Your mom doesn't have me there to hold her when you make her cry.

We went home. Home to Philly. My mother cried, and so did my father. We cried together. I don't want you to find any bad guys in this letter. I just want to make sure you will never forget where you came from and find the same joy in your relationships your mother and I found in ours. The only sad thing about our romance is that I never got to see her fully healed. She was beautiful broken. I am sure she is glorious whole.

A gliklekhe rayze, my little one! I will always be with you.

Your Father,

Daniel Aaron Eppstein

DAY 0

1/3/1986

His nails were cracked and bumpy against my skin. I rubbed his cold fingertips between my own. They were as wide as his knuckles, those knobby joints, where bending once occurred when he turned a page or opened a door. Daniel's hand was too heavy, now that it was empty of life. I held his palm to my lips, wetting it with my tears. Our baby kicked in either protest or solidarity as if to say, "Daniel was here."

DAY 1

2/28/1986

"It's a girl," Dr. Gaymen said as she passed the screaming baby to the nurse.

"A girl?" Mary left my side to follow the babe, her disbelief evident in her raised brows. Arriving at the cradle, she looked down, and Daniel's cheeks appeared in her smile. I watched as the nurse dried my baby and swaddled her.

My empty arms itched to once again be full as Mary lifted the baby and carried her to me. With the bundle settled against my breast, I looked down at her perfect little face. "Hello, Catherine."

ABOUT C.L. CABRERA

You probably know me best for my urban fantasy, I Am Armageddon, but guess what? I write more than angels.

I am a Labor and Delivery nurse and a mother of three girls from Washington state. My love of writing started in second grade and never stopped. In college, I competed in slam poetry while studying Anthropology, and then fell into the comfortable habits of an avid reader as I started my family. It took surviving Covid as a nurse for me to realize life is too short not to do what I love. So, I dove into the writing community head first and haven't come up for air yet.

ALSO BY C L CABRERA

I Am Armageddon

All nurses are angels, but not all nurses have wings. Wylie does. She just doesn't know it yet.

Reeling from the loss of her family, emergency room nurse Wylie is destined to be the catalyst of the apocalypse. As she grieves, angelic abilities surface. Wylie learns her true identity and the terrible prophecy that comes with it.

Only two men can help her now, the human doctor with whom she has an inhuman connection and the angel who has searched for her since the original sin.

With them at her side, she delves deeper into the world of angels and their fight for freedom. Soon Wylie realizes the prophecy may be a self-fulfilling one.

Armageddon Awakened

Now that Wylie knows who she is, can she leave her life behind to become the weapon she was meant to be? Will the world end on her terms or is she just another pawn? Can she move passed her grief and learn how to love again?

Armageddon Avenged

Wylie was born to be the midwife of the apocalypse, but now that the end is here, is she strong enough to lead God's Army and Humanity through it? Join Wylie as she dons the mantle of the chosen one instead of her usual scrubs.

The Heir's Querida

THE PRIDE OF THE FALLEN

C. L. CABRERA

ALSO BY C L CABRERA

THE HEIR'S QUERIDA

1 Peter 5:8 - Be sober, be vigilant; because your adversary the devil, as a roaring lion, walketh about, seeking whom he may devour

Tommy unbuttoned his jeans with shaking hands. I pulled up his undershirt, revealing his beer belly. It spilled over his belt, milky, pale, and soft.

I ran my thumb over his cheek. "Is this your first time?"

"Yes, ma'am."

I pushed him onto the bed. "Don't worry," the bed dipped as I straddled him. "I'll take care of you."

My fingers found the crevice of his neck where his pulse drummed against his skin.

He shivered, his body going rigid. I rolled my hips against him and rested my hand on his bare chest. Our eyes connected, and I drew a sip of his life force through our skin-to-skin contact. I waited for him to relax before sliding my consciousness into his skull. Slow. Inches at a time. His awareness stretched as I filled his brain with my own thoughts.

My body convulsed with pleasure, and I slipped all the way in. Waiting for my heart to steady, I studied the man's face. My invasion had emptied his eyes. "I hope that was as good for you as it was for me." I lightly smacked his cheek and climbed off, heading to my recliner in the room's corner. "Tommy?"

"Hmmm?"

"Tell me how long you've worked at the cement plant." I crossed my legs.

"Five years."

"And what do you know about the owner?" I felt bad for the bastard. He might be dirty and a little pudgy, but he loved his mama, loved his church, and volunteered at the animal shelter. It's too bad I'd be sending him off still a virgin.

"His name is Luc Devon. He's thirty-six years old, and drives a Ferrari."

"Does he have a girlfriend? Any close friends? Family?"

"Not that he brings around the plant."

The questioning went on for another thirty minutes. *Time to send him off with good memories.* I couldn't have him getting suspicious. I reached for the side table. *The Virgin Princess* fell open to page one-hundred-and-twenty-two, where I'd broken the spine. I cleared my throat and read aloud. "Their bodies moved together as he spread her legs wide . . ."

After reading Tommy his happy ending, I sent him on his way, his mind once again his own. I left my apartment moments later, my hands shoved deep in the pockets of my leather coat.

Vacation time! Satan, get me out of this shithole.

I landed in Diamond Falls three months ago, and ever since, the slow pace squeezed the life out of me. My skin crawled with claustrophobia. The small-town vibes suffocated me whenever a woman leaned over to whisper into her neighbor's ear as I walked by.

A splotch on the bible belt's buckle; this place expected its citizens to hold themselves a notch tighter than the rest of the nation. People here didn't like me. Maybe the red lipstick scandalized them. If not, my wardrobe did the job.

If only they knew.

Diamond Falls had a demon problem, and I'm not just talking about me.

Technically, I'm a succubus. Or at least that's how I registered when I joined the PPL, *or The People* as we like to call ourselves, sent me undercover in this bullshit town. The Paranormal Protection League plucked me out of the foster care system after I sucked the life out of my first girlfriend with our first kiss.

But Querida, you ask, *how can you stick out like a sore thumb and work undercover?*

Easy, they think I'm a prostitute.

If only my customers knew they were my personal food delivery service. I'd drink my fill, take their cash, read them a scene or two from my latest romance novel, and they'd leave thinking I showed them the time of their lives. Easy-peasy. Their human brains soaked up every word as I shared images of tongues and hands and thighs, of panting and sweating and fucking. They'd walk away silly with blood loss, fatigued from sharing their life force.

Diamond had more demons per capita than New York or LA, which explained why the place clutched their pearls as tight as they held onto religion. The humans adapted by grabbing for the only defense they had: God.

I resisted holding up my middle finger as I passed a church, making it to the Greyhound station just in time. *Payment, ticket, fuck you Diamond.*

While I called these monthly meetings a vacation, checking in with my handler wouldn't be cambion's play either. He likely wouldn't be impressed with my findings. We'd suspected the cement plant for a couple of weeks now, but I took the damn tour and couldn't smell anything nefarious under the sharp sting of chemicals in my sinuses. And the only thing suspicious about Luke Devon was that he's a dude with two first names.

I stepped onto the bus. My three-inch heels announced my presence. Several heads lifted. My eyes scanned the faces of the passengers. I picked the prettiest girl and slid in next to her, shoving my bag and jacket under the seat. She wore rose-colored cowboy boots and matching lipstick. *You don't belong here either, do you, sweetheart?*

"Hi. I'm Tonya, I'm heading to Tennessee. I'm going to be a country singer." She pushed her blond braid over her shoulder.

I smiled, guessing I picked a talker. "I'm sure you already are." I flashed my pearly whites and grazed her elbow with my hand. She caught her breath and leaned close. "I go by Querida."

"Nice to meet you." Her freckled nose scrunched. "You're beautiful."

Humans always reacted to my kind this way. Mesmerized. Filterless.

I ran a finger down her outer thigh. "That's nice, girlie. You're pretty." I might have kissed her neck then. *Why?* Because my kind were always hungry.

"Oh." She slumped back as I took just enough of her life force to top me off.

"Yes, oh." I smiled against her skin. *This was going to be a fun trip.* I slipped off my heels and suck in my teeth.

I woke to the sound of the bus screeching to a halt. Moonlight glowed through the windows, outlining everyone with silver. *We shouldn't be stopping yet? We aren't supposed to get to DC until the morning.*

My arms stretched up as I breathed in the emotions surrounding me. The salty smell of sleep emanated from the passengers. A hint of tangy fear wafted from the driver. The breeze from the air conditioner sending it splashing into my face. He leaned over the driver's wheel, his head swiveling on his neck as if someone rounded the front of the bus. He jerked up with a cry before slumping forward. The horn pierced the silence as he slid off the steering wheel and his seatbelt stretched tight.

None of the passengers stirred. *A sandman?* I turned to Tonya, whose head rested on my shoulder. I pinched her thigh hard. She nuzzled my neck, her eyes still closed. Now that I knew what to look for, I sucked her scent in. She smelled of magic. *Shit! Devil's spawn! Satan's staff!*

A soft snore escaped her as I pressed her against the window and ducked down laying on her lap. I wrapped my fingers around her wrist and pulled it to my teeth, just a few more gulps for strength. The accordion door screeched as someone forced it open. I licked my lips.

"She's in there. Tommy said he saw her board." A man's voice. He smelled like the sleep of the passengers. *Maybe the sandman?*

"This better not be a waste of time." The voice that answered reverberated in my chest and then my lower belly and thighs. He smelled like leather and bourbon and pine and incubus but stronger. My mouth watered. *A lot stronger.*

Banshee fucker! I ignored my body's natural response to the demon's power and closed my eyes.

"Wait out here. Her powers won't work on me." Again that smooth bass. Well, it didn't matter if my powers worked or not, I could defend myself in other ways. I slipped a dagger from the holster under my shirt and closed my eyes at the sound of boots climbing the steps. *I'm supposed to be on vacation.*

I held in my sigh of relief as I heard the man walk past me. The metal crunched with each step, the sound becoming louder again as he turned from the back of the bus.

"There you are."

Big hands pulled me out of my seat, his fingers curling around my rib cage. My back hit his chest as I planted my dagger in his thigh. Blood gushed.

"Shit!" He released me and I lept forward. The collar of my shirt cut into my throat, choking me. He dragged me against him, holding tight to the fabric with one hand and grabbing a handful of my hair with the other. "Now stay still, brat."

"Go to hell."

He snorted, a puff of his breath combing the back of my ear. I threw my head back, and his nose crunched under the blow. With one swift move, I removed my dagger from his thigh and cut off my hair. My shirt went next and freedom.

I shot out of the bus in nothing but a bra and a miniskirt. Demon blood crusted my dagger hand, and an icy wind bit at my naked skin. I melted into the darkness, jumping off the road and into the tree line. I dodged shrubs and fallen branches, using my nose to choose which direction to run. A light flashed behind me, and I made the mistake of looking back.

"Shit!" I glimpsed at his bloodied face for a split second before I ran into the wall of his chest.

His arms wrapped around me. "Hey, brat, I thought I told you to stay still." He lifted me off my feet. "Now, Shafer."

The sandman's magic hit me in the back at full force, knocking the breath out of me. I sank into the male who held me, my vision blinking out, and the cotton sensation of his magic clogging my brain. I was too strong for the bastard to put to sleep. If only my body could realize that. My legs hung limp. The male holding me adjusted me in his arms. My cheek fell against his peck, bouncing with every step.

Lucifer's balls! I don't have time for this.

"Luc, man, slow the fuck down. I'm running on empty."

Wait, is this Luc Devon? Maybe I do have time for this. Did I just fall into my target's lap?

"Do you need me to carry you too?" The rumble in Luke's chest as he spoke vibrated against my cheek. If I had control of my body, I would be crossing my legs. *Hey, bad guy, do you mind repeating that while I'm sitting on your face?*

"I'm just saying, we've got her. There's no race."

Fingers pushed my hair from my face. "She doesn't look anything like Tommy described."

Of course, I don't, dumbass. When you look at a succubi . . .

"When you look at a Succubi, you see what you want to see."

"How do you know?" Asphalt crunched under us, my ride growing smoother.

"My cousin married one. Let's just say when I found out the homely chick in the wedding photo was the bride I danced with, I was floored. He thought he was marrying a young Megan Fox but ended up with Sarah Jessica Parker after a beating with an ugly stick."

If he's related to you, sandman, she probably married up.

I absorbed Luc's chuckle. "Are they still married?"

"Twenty plus years. To each their own." A car security system chirped. "Here, let me get the trunk."

The trunk? My heart raced at the prospect. *Please don't put me in there.* Memories of dark nights locked in small spaces itched at my skin.

"Nah, you drive. I'll ride in the back with her."

"Are you sure?"

"Shut up and open the door."

Yeah, Shaf, shut the fuck up.

Luke climbed in, buckled his seatbelt, and keeping me cradled against him, rolled down the window.

What no seatbelt for me, buddy?

The engine hiccupped to life, and Shafer revved it like an idoit.

"It's cold. What's up with the window."

"She's hot. I'm sweating back here."

You're right, I am hot.

"Another reason she should be in the trunk."

Go suck satan's staff, Shaf.

"I'm tired of your shit tonight, Shafer."

Yeah Luc, way to stand up for me.

"I'm just saying, when we're done finding out why the PPL's following us, we're going to have to put her down. It's best not to get attached."

Put me down? Like I'm a puppy or something? What's he talking about, Luc?

"Have I ever had a problem with that?"

My fingers curled around his sleeve, and I forced my eyes open.

"She's not asleep."

I couldn't manage much else, so I glared as hard as I could. I couldn't see any outward sign of what demon type he belonged to. Neatly parted black hair, heavy brows, thick lips, strong jaw, damn this man was the whole package, too bad he planned to kill me.

"Hey, brat, are you awake?" A smile pulled at his cheeks as I studied his moss and oak colored eyes.

"Stop playing with your food, Luc."

Luke pulled me tighter to his chest, his chin lifting. "I'm getting really tired of you telling me what to do."

"You're acting weird tonight."

"Well, I did get stabbed."

True, true. He did get stabbed.

"Don't be an imp."

Yeah, Luc, stop your whining, I didn't stab you that hard.

"Fuck you."

"Maybe after I'm done with your mama."

"Your mama jokes dont work on me. Plus, when my father spawned me, he was fucking your mama. So, we're basically brothers."

If only I could roll my eyes.

"You've met my mother."

"I've also known her."

"Stop, please." The car swerved at the sound of my voice.

"Shit, she is awake."

"I told you."

"I'm surrounded by idiots." My body still wouldn't move. "I'm not going to talk. You might as well just throw me out of the window so I can finish freezing to death."

"Trust me, brat, you'll talk."

"Trust me, ass, I wont."

Luc leaned forward, his nose at my hairline. "She doesn't smell like succubus. Are you sure that's what she is?"

"Well, now I'm not sure either. That blast should've knocked her out for days."

"You mean that tickle."

"Can you do it again, so she'll shut up?"

"I'm driving, why don't you do your thing?"

"His thing?" I sucked in a breath. "Not his thing. Oh, no."

"I bet you're wishing you put her in the trunk now."

"You could always pull over."

"No. No. No. I'm good. I'll be good."

"Like you know how."

"Shut up, Sandman."

"That's it, I'm pulling over."

The car swerved again and the tire squealed as he hit the brakes.

I pulled Luc's sleeve, my eye boring into his. "Please, please don't put me in the trunk. I'll be good."

"Come on, Shaf, did you hear that? She said she'd be good." Luc pushed open the door as he spoke.

"Luc, please. I can't move. Please."

"You heard the driver. Brats get the trunk."

My hip hit first, then my head, and the truck lid slammed shut. I screamed, memories instantly flooded my brain.

Someone's foot landed in my belly. Holy oil splashed over my face, stinging my eyes. The closet door crunched my fingers again and again. And then the words came.

"Saint Michael, the Archangel, defend us in battle; be our protection against the wickedness and snares of the devil."

My fingers and my ribs throbbed, but I beat on the door with my fists, screaming every curse word I knew. My child-mind knew I was going to die.

"May God rebuke him, we humbly pray. And do thou, O Prince of the Heavenly Host, by the Power of God, thrust into hell Satan and

all the evil spirits who wander through the world seeking the ruin of souls. Amen."

And that's when they threw the lit match inside.

"Fuck. Is she dying?" The trunk opened, and Luke lifted me.

"What's wrong with her?" The sandman's hand rested on my forehead for a split second before he yanked it back. I felt my memories trail behind his touch as if he pulled them out. "Shit, humans. Hell, I'm sorry."

"What?" Luke looked from me to Shafer. "What?"

"Here, let me get her to sleep. She'll let me this time. Right, angel?"

I nodded, unable to make a smartass remark if I wanted to. His hand covered my eyes, and warmth and oblivion spread through me.

www.ingramcontent.com/pod-product-compliance
Lightning Source LLC
LaVergne TN
LVHW091010080826
845145LV00003B/1205

* 9 7 8 1 9 6 3 7 5 5 0 2 2 *